Creating Your Career Portfolio

At-a-Glance Guide for Students
Third Edition

Anna Graf Williams Ph.D.
Karen J. Hall

PEARSON
Prentice
Hall

Prentice Hall
Upper Saddle River, NJ 07458

Library of Congress Cataloging-in-Publication Data

TX
911.3
.V62
W53
2005

Williams, Anna Graf.
    Creating your career portfolio: at a glance guide for students / Anna Graf Williams,
Karen J. Hall.--3rd ed.
        p. cm.
    Includes index.
    ISBN 0-13-150504-1
    1. Hospitality industry--Vocational guidance. I. Hall, Karen J. II. Title.

TX911.3.V62W53 2005
647.94'023--dc22

2003068938

Executive Editor: Stephen Helba	**Media Coordinator:** Lisa Rinaldi
Executive Editor: Vernon R. Anthony	**Manufacturing Buyer:** Cathleen Petersen
Executive Assistant: Nancy Kesterson	**Creative Director:** Cheryl Asherman
Editorial Assistant: Ann Brunner	**Cover Coordinator:** Christopher Weigand
Managing Editor: Mary Carnis	**Marketing Manager:** Ryan DeGrote
Production Editor: Linda Zuk/ WordCrafters	**Marketing Assistant:** Elizabeth Farrell
	Marketing Coordinator: Adam Kloza
Production Liaison: Adele M. Kupchik	**Printer/Binder:** R.R. Donnelley & Sons Co.
Development Editor: Anna Graf Williams	
Interior Design: Karen J. Hall	**Cover Illustration:** Learnovation®, LLC
Composition: Learnovation®, LLC	**Cover Printer:** Phoenix Color Corp.
Director of Manufacturing and Production: Bruce Johnson	

Pearson Education LTD.
Pearson Education Singapore, Pte. Ltd
Pearson Education, Canada, Ltd
Pearson Education–Japan

Pearson Education Australia PTY, Limited
Pearson Education North Asia Ltd
Pearson Educación de Mexico, S.A. de C.V.
Pearson Education Malaysia, Pte. Ltd

10 9 8 7 6 5 4 3 2 1

ISBN 0-13-150504-1

To everyone who is looking to package who they **really** are...
may you find hope and professional success
in pursuit of the portfolio process.

CONTENTS

PREFACE

If you're looking to find the right job, stand out among the competition, prove yourself, and feel confident in the interview process, you are ready to create your career portfolio.

Succeed in a tough job market—Use your career portfolio to compete for the job, show your future employer what you are worth and how you can save them training dollars. Show that employer you are worth the investment!

Stand Out—With the help of this book you are going to create a Career Portfolio, a track record of your education and work experiences that you can take with you to a job interview. The portfolio is a zippered 3-ring binder containing information about your beliefs, experiences, and education. It will contain samples of your work, either in a classroom setting or on the job. The portfolio may also include a list of your skills and abilities. With a portfolio in hand, you can walk into an interview and be able to show the interviewer samples of your work, pictures of projects or community involvement, certificates you've earned, and memberships you have held. Your portfolio will be customized to you, so it will set you apart from everyone else.

Interview with Confidence—A portfolio also lets you walk into an interview with more confidence, because while putting it together you'll be examining your goals, writing down your beliefs about work and your career, documenting your strengths, and identifying your weaknesses. By the time you have put together your first career portfolio you should be able to handle those hard interview questions like "Tell me about yourself," "What are your goals for the future?," or "What do you bring to the table for us?"

Start Out Ahead—Portfolios can do more than boost your confidence in an interview. They can also help you get ahead in the marketplace. A well-crafted portfolio shows employers you have the skills and abilities they are looking for. We have seen people with portfolios obtain higher starting salaries because they could prove their skills to an employer.

Track Your Career—Once you have the job, your portfolio doesn't go into a closet until you're looking for another job. Your portfolio changes as you begin to collect and document your work on the job. Then your portfolio serves as proof of your abilities on the job and can be used to track job performance and help position you for advancement.

Creating Your Career Portfolio—At-a-Glance Guide for Students, 3nd Edition, gives you guidelines for creating your career portfolio. In this book you'll find:

- **A list of supplies you need to begin**
- **General guidelines for organizing your portfolio**
- **Detailed discussions of information to be included in different sections**
- **Pointers on using the portfolio in an interview or job review**
- **A style guide—containing tips for creating better looking text, photographs, and videos, as well as other ideas for making the production side of the portfolio process run smoothly.**

Organization

This book is divided into six sections:

Overview

> **Chapter 1: The Portfolio Process**—An overview of the whole process of portfolio development.

Planning and Collecting Materials

> **Chapter 2: Planning Your Portfolio**—Tools to help you develop your work philosophy and career goals.
> **Chapter 3: The Résumé: An Overview of Your Portfolio**—A look at different types of résumés, both paper and electronic.
> **Chapter 4: Proving Your Skills**—How to collect, select, and assemble your work samples, certifications, and community service items.

Putting the Portfolio Together

> **Chapter 5: The Assembly**—Putting it all together; producing the portfolio.

Chapter 6: The Electronic Portfolio—Creating a digital version of your portfolio for the Internet or distribution on Compact Disk (CD).

How to Use the Completed Portfolio

Chapter 7: The Portfolio in Action: Getting the Job—"Now that I have it, what do I do with it?" Using the portfolio in an interview or to get an internship or co-op experience.

Making the Portfolio Look Good

Chapter 8: A Matter of Style—Production tips focusing on making your documents, pictures, and videos look their best.

Quick Reference Materials

Chapter 9: Resource Guide—Additional resources to make your career portfolio a success, including:

- Supply list with product numbers
- Emergency assembly instructions
- A list of action verbs for use in résumés
- Skill competencies
- Transferable skill list
- A list of templates included on the diskette.

We've tried to make this *At-a-Glance Guide* live up to its name. If you like to read books straight through from the beginning, you'll find this book organized in a logical way. If you don't like to read a guide until you need help with a particular step, you're in luck. You don't have to read this book from cover to cover to find helpful information. You'll find an overview to the process in this chapter. Along the way you'll see bright ideas, samples, "Ask the Expert" questions, and stories to help you make the most of the career portfolio process.

When you are ready to work on a particular portion of the portfolio, look up the specific section in Chapters 2–4 for more information.

For assistance on developing good-looking work samples and documents, refer to Chapter 8—A Matter of Style.

When you're ready to put your portfolio together, turn to Chapter 5—The Assembly, or Chapter 6—The Electronic Portfolio.

Before you go to your interview or job review, re-read Chapter 7—The Portfolio in Action...Getting the Job.

Regardless of how you use this book, you'll find it filled with examples, tips, and ideas that will make the portfolio process truly rewarding.

We have been researching from the employer and employee perspective for more than 10 years on Career Portfolios. For more hints, stories, seminar information, questions, and additional resources for the career portfolio, please check out our website at **http://learnovation.com**. If you have any questions or we can be of assistance, please feel free to contact us via mail or e-mail.

Learnovation® LLC
My Portfolio
PO Box 502150
Indianapolis, IN 46250

317-577-1190 / Fax: 317-598-0816
E-mail: **portfolio@learnovation.com**

We wish you the best of luck and success in creating your portfolio and developing your career!

CHAPTER 1

THE PORTFOLIO PROCESS

Five or ten years ago, if you were carrying a portfolio to an interview, you were probably an artist. These people carried around samples of their work in big, bulky folios. To the artist, his or her work and the skill behind it, the style and talents, were on display in the contents of the portfolio. To know the contents of his or her portfolio was to know the artist, the person behind the art.

Employers Want Proof

Today, in the extremely competitive job market of the new millennium, with many highly qualified people competing for the same jobs, employers are looking for new ways to distinguish the excellent people from the average. Having a degree is no longer considered proof of your knowledge, skills, and abilities. Employers are beginning to ask to see results; they want to see physical evidence that shows you possess the abilities you claim. Individuals are also trying to find new ways to distinguish themselves from the rest of the competitors, to find an edge. The career portfolio is designed to do just that: to provide proof of your abilities and produce a tool that is distinctly you.

The portfolio you create through this process will show the best of your work, your accomplishments, and your skills to eager employers. As the artist's portfolio showed the person behind the art, so will your portfolio show the person behind the work samples. The portfolio also includes other support material including lists of documented skills you possess, awards and achievements you've earned, letters of recommendation you've received, your goals for your future, and your vision and beliefs for the future of your industry.

Once you find "the" job, it doesn't mean your portfolio should be thrown into the dark recesses of your closet, only to be resurrected when you want to begin looking for another position. The portfolio is designed to transition with you into your job. As you continue to collect work samples and proof of your experiences on the job, you can turn your portfolio into a useful tool during a job evaluation or promotion review. Think of the impact you will have when you enter a review, fully prepared to show proof of your accomplishments over the last period!

In this chapter, we will provide you with all the basic information you need to create a career portfolio as we answer these questions:

Why do I need a portfolio?

What's in a portfolio?

What supplies do I need to get started?

How do I put it together?

How will I use this in the job search process?

How can I use this in a job review?

Step 1: Make a career plan.

Step 2: Gather work samples, certificates, letters, projects, photos, etc.

Step 3: Update résumé and references; create support materials.

Step 4: Purchase supplies & assemble the portfolio.

Step 5: Use the portfolio in an interview or review.

The Career Portfolio Process

Why Do I Need a Portfolio?

It's Proof

In an interview or review setting, a career portfolio provides proof of your skills and abilities. Instead of just talking about what you can do during an interview or job review, you can show the person your portfolio—filled with work samples you've created, lists of skills you possess, letters of recommendation, and your professional goals.

An Edge

Recruiters and managers are still not used to seeing portfolios every day. While your portfolio contains samples of your work, it also contains important information about you as a person. You can start interesting conversations that wouldn't be possible without a portfolio in hand. In some cases, having a portfolio can make it easier to stress your strengths in different areas.

It's a Process

The most important thing to remember about portfolio development is that it's a **process**. Of course, the physical portfolio is important, but **the time and effort you put into its development is the true investment in your career**.

Assembling and organizing samples of your work, developing your management philosophy and career goals, and determining the skills and competencies you want to emphasize or obtain in a job situation are key to the production of the portfolio. You can use the portfolio to track the skills you have and the ones you want to possess. As you work through these areas, you begin to examine your experiences and education from different viewpoints. You learn to recognize your strengths, and find ways to emphasize these through the portfolio. You also are faced with your weaknesses, and, in the process, you find ways to compensate. This process of examining yourself while developing the portfolio can build your confidence, so that there is little, or nothing, an interviewer or recruiter can ask you that you haven't already thought about.

A Disclaimer

Keep in mind... we don't claim that having a career portfolio is the ultimate answer to your job search. Jobs aren't going to fall out of the sky at your feet if you just raise your portfolio above your head. Developing a portfolio will help you get organized and prepared for the job market. During this process you will be examining your wants, your skills, your abilities, your strengths, and your weaknesses. This should help you feel more confident in your ability to successfully negotiate an interview. Having a neat, well-organized portfolio also projects a professional image back onto you.

While many of the examples in this book take an interviewing approach to portfolio use, don't forget the portfolio can be a critical tool in job performance reviews and internal job shifting.

What Is a Portfolio?

By this time, you may be telling yourself that it sounds like there's a lot of work involved in this portfolio process. "Analyzing yourself, collecting samples, writing goals..., can't I just hire someone to do all this work for me?"

The Average Job Search Tools

First, stop and think about the materials the "average" person creates to get ready for the job search process:

- **Résumé**
- **List of references**
- **Cover letter.**

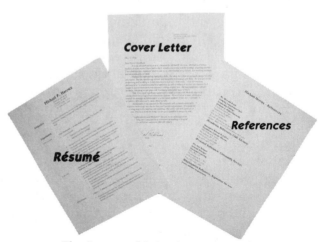

The "average" interview accessories: cover letter, résumé, and references.

All too often, these are the only materials people prepare and take with them to an interview. We are taught to believe our résumé is the key component of the interview process. Write a good cover letter that explains why you are perfect for this organization, include a nicely formatted résumé that shows education and work experience, include some activities and achievements to trigger their curiosity, and you are done with the process.

Make sure you bring a list of people who will say nice things about you to serve as references and you are ready. Keep in mind the cover letter, résumé, and references are important tools in the job search process. **The résumé and cover letter are the tools you use to get your foot in the door for an interview.** They summarize your abilities and explain why you are well suited to the position. They aren't as helpful during the actual interview, except as a reference for the interviewer.

The Career Portfolio

Now, the person with a Career Portfolio brings a zippered 3-ring binder to the interview containing a combination of the following tabbed sections:

Statement of Originality	A paragraph stating this is your work and asking them to keep it confidential.
Work Philosophy	A brief description of your beliefs about yourself and the industry.
Career Goals	Your professional goals for the next two to five years.
Résumé	A brief summary of your education and experiences.
Skill Areas	Tabbed sections containing information on the different types of skills you want to promote such as Management, Marketing, Training, Technology, Communications, etc.

Each skill area may contain:

Work Samples
Physical examples of your work. Projects, reports, documents, pictures, etc. Work samples show your skills in this area.

Letters of Recommendation
Letters of support or reference from people who can verify your abilities in this skill area.

Skill Sets
Checklists of critical skills related to this area. As you attain different levels of competency with each skill, an instructor or employer can sign off on your ability to perform the skill. These are usually pre-existing checklists of skills standardized by an organization.

Works in Progress
A brief list of work, activities, projects, or efforts you are in the process of completing.

Certifications, Diplomas, Degrees, and Awards
Copies of certifications, diplomas, and degrees earned. Copies of special awards and recognitions you have received. Include documentation used to track skills attained for certification.

Community Service
Work samples, letters of recognition, photos of projects completed, programs and brochures relating to community service projects.

Professional Memberships and Certifications
Membership cards, citations, and letters related to professional organizations.

Academic Plan of Study
A copy of your plan of study that lists courses you have taken to fulfill your degree.

Faculty and Employer Biographies	Brief descriptions of the people whose names appear throughout the portfolio—who they are and what they do.
References	A list of people who can verify your character, academic record, or employment history.

The Career Portfolio

Now, which person do you think looks more prepared for the interview—the one with the average tools or a career portfolio?

What Supplies Do I Need to Get Started?

The materials you use to create the portfolio serve two purposes:

1. To help organize your materials and documents so you can easily customize your portfolio for a given interview or review period.

2. To make your portfolio look professional. A quick shopping list of supplies, including brands and product numbers, is found in Chapter 9, Resource Guide.

Portfolio Supplies

Purchase These Supplies

Here is a list of supplies that will help you begin the process of collecting and assembling your portfolio:

- **Plastic file tote box**—(1 to 2 boxes) Used to store work samples, materials, etc. Should be able to hold hanging file folders.

- **Hanging file folders**—20 to 30 folders.

- **Zippered 3-ring notebook**—Cloth, leather, or vinyl with 1-1/2" to 2" rings. Cloth is the cheapest, ranging from $7–$20. Vinyl costs $20–$30, and leather binders often run $60 or higher. All are available at local office supply stores.

- **Sheet protectors**—Clear, plastic, 3-hole punched pockets that hold documents and work samples. They protect your portfolio and give it a professional look. Avoid the non-glare variety because they are harder to read.

- **Connected sheet protectors**—Three to five sets of sheet protectors, bound together in sets of 5 or 10 sheets. These are great for keeping projects and work samples neatly together in your file box. This makes it easier to swap work samples in and out of the portfolio.

- **Extra-wide 3-ring tabs with labels**—Page protectors are wider than ordinary 3-ring tabs. You need to find extra-wide tabs made for use with page protectors.

- **Paper**—Use a high quality paper. See Chapter 8, A Matter of Style, for suggestions on paper choices.
- **Business cards**—Blank sheets of cards are used to create overview cards for work samples. You don't have to use plain white cards—select something that shows your style.
- **Photo sheet holders**—Plastic sheets that can hold vertical and/or horizontal pictures.
- **Nameplate or vinyl card holder**—Used on the cover of the portfolio to identify it as your property.
- **Zippered pouch—(optional)** Holds videos.
- **Diskette holders—(optional)** Holds project diskettes.

A more detailed list, including brands and product numbers, can be found in Chapter 9, Resource Guide.

Have Access to This Equipment

A professional portfolio looks good and feels good. To make this portfolio something you can be proud of, you should plan on using the following equipment when you create documents and work samples to enhance the quality of your career portfolio:

- **Computer**—You should have access to current versions of word processor, graphic presentation, and spreadsheet packages.
- **Printer**—Laser or high-quality ink jet.
- **Color flatbed scanner**—Used to scan certificates, work samples, etc.
- **Color copier or color printer**—Used to reproduce work samples, certificates, awards, etc.
- **Film camera or digital camera**—Used for photographing work samples and documenting other activities.
- **Video camera**—Videotape yourself in action when necessary.

Things You Don't Need

- **Ink pens**—Do everything on a computer.
- **3-hole paper punch**—Use page protectors instead of punching holes. Your work will look more professional.

- **Paper clips, staples, and tape**—If you want to connect several pages or display a work sample, use a set of connected sheet protectors.

Creating and Using the Portfolio

A Little Planning Goes a Long Way

Getting the supplies together to produce your portfolio is the easy part. Deciding what to put into your portfolio requires planning and organization. Begin by analyzing your strengths and weaknesses. What are you best at? Which skills and abilities do you want to emphasize? Are there things you'd rather not have people ask about, or skills you know you are lacking but would like to have? Taking the time to examine your experiences and abilities will help you focus on your key skill areas you will use in your portfolio. You will also use the planning time to write your work philosophy and career goals. A **work philosophy** gives an employer a unique perspective on you as a person through your personal beliefs about work and your industry. **Career goals** show the employer you have a plan for your life.

 Bright Idea!

Save everything you create! You can decide which samples to use later when you're ready to assemble your portfolio.

Collect and Organize Work Samples

Once you have decided on your key skill areas, you need to find things that demonstrate your abilities in each area. You can use projects, reports, photos, letters of recommendation, certificates, newspaper articles, and any materials you have created on the job, in school, or through community service.

Putting the Portfolio Together

When you are ready to assemble your portfolio, you will gather your supplies, along with a good friend (this is very important!!), and choose the samples to use.

- Decide what key skill areas you want to focus on and create a **tab page** for each. Then pick three or four of your best samples for each area and put them into sheet protectors or photo holders.

- Create **work sample overview cards** for each sample to help a viewer quickly identify the type of sample and what it represents. The card is slid into the sheet protector and floats over the top of the sample.

- Create a **statement of originality and confidentiality** to indicate this is your work.

- Print out your **work philosophy** and **career goals**, your **résumé** and **references**.

- Create a list of **works in progress** to indicate projects you are working on now for which you have no work samples.

- Create a list of your professional **memberships** and create a **Faculty and Employer Bio Sheet** listing information about the people mentioned in your portfolio.

- Put copies of your **certificates** and **awards** in sheet protectors, along with an **academic plan of study** if you want to stress your course work.

- Set up and print out the **tabs** and insert them in the dividers.

As you are assembling your portfolio, be sure to reference the Style Guide in Chapter 8 for tips on making your portfolio look its best. Once you put your portfolio together, you're ready to put it to good use.

Using the Portfolio in the Job Search Process

So, how do you put the portfolio to work? Remember, it's your résumé that helps get you the interview. Once you have an interview scheduled, you'll want to make sure the samples in your portfolio show you to the best advantage. Each employer is looking for different things, and you may need to use different work samples to prove different skills. Customize your portfolio for the interview.

During the interview you can use your portfolio to answer questions or show examples of your work. Just by having a portfolio along, you can show the interviewer you have organization skills and are focused on your career. Your portfolio can make a lasting impression. Some people have also sent copies of their portfolio along with the thank-you letter after an interview to reinforce their skills, especially when they didn't have a chance to fully use their portfolio during the interview itself.

How Will I Use a Portfolio in a Job Review?

If you already have a job and you want to shine in a performance review or want to have an edge in the promotion process, you can use your portfolio to keep track of what you have accomplished and present it in an organized manner.

James's Story

James was feeling a little down after his interview. The interviewer hadn't seemed too interested in his portfolio and he had really wanted to show him some of the things he had created on the job. James went to the copy shop and made a spiral-bound color copy of his portfolio. He sent the copy to the interviewer with his thank-you letter. In the letter he asked the interviewer to take a few minutes and glance at the portfolio, being sure to point out some of the highlights.

James's extra effort made the difference. The interviewer did take the time to look through his portfolio and was impressed by what he saw. James was called back for a second interview and got the job and a larger starting salary based on the contents of his career portfolio.

Steps for Growing Your Career

You can use your portfolio on the job to keep track of what you have done and what you plan to do in the next quarter. Here are some ideas of things to record:

- Keep a listing of projects and documents you have completed during the last review period.
- Keep track of the committees and projects you've worked with.
- Set goals for each review period and track your achievements. Show how your goals help meet the goals of the company.
- Include any community service activities in which you have been involved.
- If necessary, update your work philosophy and your career goals, both outside and within the company.
- Keep copies of thank-you letters and memos that document teamwork or cooperation.
- If your supervisor is new, you should include highlights of your career since you were hired by the company.
- Let your supervisor know well in advance of your review that you are using a career portfolio.

Before Your Review

Talk with your boss an d explain the contents of your portfolio. Drop off the portfolio a few days before your review so he or she has time to review it. Then discuss it at your annual review.

Kathy's Job Review

Kathy's boss was a little intimidated by her portfolio. When she saw the updated résumé and references, she was sure she was ready to look for a job. Kathy assured her that her portfolio was a "career" portfolio, tracking her performance and abilities on the job. Keeping it up to date showed her organization skills and helped her track her goals and achievements.

How Will I Use a Portfolio in an Internal Job Shift?

The portfolio can be a great help if you are looking to advance or to shift laterally within a company. People job shift inside a company in order to change their responsibilities, find new growth opportunities, or obtain salary increases. An up-to-date portfolio can help you position yourself where you want to be.

Your portfolio needs to contain samples of your accomplishments in your department. You should also include samples that show your management skills of people or projects. Make sure you note any committees or special projects you have been involved in, and highlight your product knowledge and transferable skills.

Transferable Skills and Job Shifting

George was a technical writer in the company, writing documentation and manuals for a software program. When a position opened up in the Training Development area of the company to create training for the same programs, he applied. In his portfolio, he highlighted his current experience with the company, his extensive product knowledge, and writing ability. He used his portfolio to document his training experience and educational background in training and emphasized skills he could use in both positions.

Using the Portfolio to Keep Track of Certifications and Professional Development

A portfolio is a great tool for managing information. More organizations are beginning to use portfolios to keep track of member progress toward industry certification. Many people use a portfolio only for tracking things they've accomplished; others use it as a means of assessment, where the contents of the portfolio indicate the success of the program.

The portfolio can be a tool for tracking your progress toward specific certification in your field. Whether you are working to

become a certified CPA, Novell administrator, or Registered Die-
tician, you can use the career portfolio as a place to track your
progress toward your goal. Depending on your certification process, you may have a structured set of materials that you can
put into the portfolio where you can list or mark down what you
have accomplished to date. If no formal plan fits, you can create
your own forms and lists to track your progress.

Remember, the portfolio isn't just for getting a new job; it's a
tool for tracking your skills and abilities. As you obtain new
skills, you should add them to the portfolio. Keep this document up to date, and you'll be ready for anything.

Sounds Great—But It Won't Work for Me

"Sounds great but it won't work for me." If there is something in
your gut that makes you uneasy with the prospect of developing
a portfolio, there are two possible explanations. First, you may
be a master procrastinator and this is your normal response to
work efforts. The second, and more likely, possibility is that you
can't see yourself with enough work samples to make the portfolio process work.

Common Stumbling Blocks

- Lack of physical work samples
- Unclear personal goals
- Not sure how to use the portfolio in your particular industry
  or profession.

Throughout the development of this portfolio process, several
people kept telling us— "this sounds great but..." We kept trying to figure out the reasons for their resistance to the process.
Was it too much work? Were they unsure about how to actually
use it in an interview? Finally, after observing one person's
struggle during a full-time job search, we discovered the problem.

The Portfolio in Action

Our friend George wanted a different job and had background and experience to do many different kinds of work. George had a solid, formal education and lots of community service background, but he kept blocking when we offered to help him put together the portfolio. This went on for months. Then all of a sudden, one employer said, "Could you do a presentation for us and bring us some of your work to the interview tomorrow?" We followed the guidelines for the "Emergency Portfolio" in Chapter 9, Resource Guide, and helped him create a portfolio for the next day. He admitted that "A portfolio was the best way to organize my work."

George found that the process wasn't so bad, and the portfolio worked well in the interview. When we quizzed him about what kept him from doing it earlier, he said, "Most of the résumés I sent out were for jobs where I didn't have an exact match to the company." He felt the portfolio worked best when he could match his work samples to the skills needed by the company.

The story continues. In subsequent interviews he used his portfolio each time. George said, "Most people conducting the interview don't know how to get information out of you. This portfolio stuff works because you can prompt the interviewer to ask better questions." In several interviews, George found the interviewer wasn't very interested in the portfolio at the beginning of the interview, but when he used it to answer a question about his experience, it piqued the interviewer's curiosity enough to look through the whole portfolio. Every time he was asked how well the portfolio worked, he would say, "It blew them away—they were impressed."

We're happy to say George found a job where his talents and experiences could be well used. "I might have still gotten this job without it," he said, "but the portfolio made the interview go more smoothly. The interviewers were impressed by the portfolio, and it made me a more visible candidate. At my 90-day review I learned I had started about $5,000 higher than average because I had the portfolio and could show them my skills." The moral of the story is... if you are feeling overwhelmed and uneasy about the portfolio, be sure you are seeking out positions that are really you.

I Don't Need a Portfolio; I Have Lots of Job Offers

"The job market is real good right now and I have lots of offers." If this sounds like you—congratulations! It would be easy to take the path of least resistance here. Consider, however, that using the portfolio may help to "up the offer." Remember that getting the job is the first hurdle, keeping it is the next, followed by the goal of getting promoted and rewarded for the job.

Upping the Offer

When you have a portfolio, you have your professional goals spelled out. You can use this section, along with your work samples, to get more money or better benefits. Pam developed her portfolio, after receiving three offers, to help justify her negotiations for benefits and perks. The money being offered may be preset, but the benefits package can often be expanded for secondary benefits. Secondary benefits are the non-insurance and retirement benefits. She used her portfolio to demonstrate her abilities and her need for professional development. Each of these companies agreed to pay for her professional memberships and one three-day professional meeting. This would save her an average of $1,200 out-of-pocket expenses per year. She was also able to convince her eventual employer to purchase an additional copy of the software they used in the office for home use. This made her job easier by having the same software at home to do her work.

There is something about the portfolio process which causes you to reflect on who you are, what you want to do, and to search out what you are good at doing. Let's focus on getting you rewarded for your work. Using the portfolio process for upping the offer in the interview sets you up to use it on the job during your performance appraisals or year-end reviews.

 Bright Idea!

Use a portfolio as a bargaining tool when you have lots of job offers.

I Need a Portfolio Now!!!

"Oh, it won't take that long to put it together."

"I have one that I used last time."

"My interview is tomorrow and I have to do all this before I can start on my portfolio?"

"Help, I have an interview tomorrow and they asked me to bring work samples!"

If you've just purchased this book and want to put together a portfolio for an interview tomorrow morning, or if you've had this book for a while and suddenly your interview is upon you, there's still hope. Based on several frantic experiences of our own, rest assured you can put together a basic career portfolio in three hours if you have a computer, printer, and your best friend's help. See Chapter 9, Resource Guide, for all the details on creating the emergency portfolio.

Read On

You now have the basic ideas necessary to create your portfolio. In the following chapters you will learn how to plan and organize your portfolio and make a personalized tool for career success.

We've organized these sections as you would position them in the completed portfolio. This doesn't mean you will be developing your materials in this order; quite the contrary, you have to make the most of the opportunities at hand. You'll probably be saving projects and papers or securing signatures for skill areas long before you focus on your résumé. Refer to Chapter 5, Assembly, for tips on organizing and creating the actual portfolio.

Keep in mind as you continue through this book that a portfolio provides:

Insight into you as a person

- Statement of Originality & Confidentiality
- Work Philosophy

- Goals.

A summary of your portfolio

- Résumé.

Proof of your abilities

- Skill Areas containing:
  - Work Samples
  - Letters of Recommendation
  - Skill Sets
  - Community Service
  - Certifications, Awards, Degrees, and Diplomas
  - Works in Progress.

Your commitment to your own personal and professional growth

- Professional Memberships
- Professional Development Plans.

Reference materials

- Academic Plan of Study
- Faculty and Employer Bios
- References.

CHAPTER 2

PLANNING YOUR PORTFOLIO

If you could have anything in your life, what would you want? This is the place where you begin to evaluate your work philosophy and establish goals. This chapter will provide you with the mechanics and several tools for generating the pieces you need in your portfolio. You analyze current and yet-to-be acquired skills. This is where you design your career. Keep in mind your career is more than a job—it's the paths those jobs take.

This is a process you do when you are looking for a job, and where you should go three to four months into the job to connect with the corporate culture and company goals.

Designing Your Career

You've got to have a goal. If you don't, your career will be one reaction after another. With a plan in place from your master design, you're able to maintain your focus. You may encounter opportunities or career shifts or additional training. With your career goals in mind, you can determine which opportunities to accept and which to decline. This is the part of the process where you get a master plan. Be sure you hold a higher vision of your potential when you do it.

Work Philosophy

A work philosophy is a statement of your beliefs about yourself, people, and your outlook on life in your industry. Your work philosophy is often used by an interviewer to see if you match a company's corporate culture. After reading this statement, a potential employer should know whether you would fit the "style" of the organization.

Try This with a Friend...

Have both your friend and yourself list five adjectives that describe who you are and how you want to be seen in the workplace. Use a friend to react to your list. Do they agree? Use these adjectives to guide your work philosophy statement, serving as the core thoughts and keywords.

Make sure you have a friend to assist you when you're ready to develop your work philosophy. Your friend can help you take your beliefs and the ideas that you have internalized and verbalize them on paper. Many people know in their hearts what they believe, but they've never put it into words. Your work philosophy might also be called a management philosophy.

What you need to know about your philosophy...

- **Think about it**—Don't expect to "whip out" a work philosophy or personal mission statement in 10 or 20 minutes. It usually takes a few days worth of thought and reflection before the "final draft" is ready.

- **Place your most important belief first**—Your work philosophy should be unique to you, communicate who you are and what makes you different from others who may want the same position.

- **Length**—Your work philosophy should be one to four sentences in length, and should address your beliefs and your outlook on people.

- **Use bullets**—Consider using bullet points for added clarity.

- **Have a friend review it for clarity**—After you have it on paper, ask a few friends to read it for clarity—not approval. Remember, your work philosophy is never right or wrong; it represents your key beliefs and values.

Here's the work philosophy of one graduating student:

Work Philosophy

- The customer always comes first.
- Financial and operational controls must be clear to all members of the company.
- Technology will be critical in reaching the guests and communicating within the company.
- I want to be part of a winning team.

 Template

Use the **Work Philosophy and Goals.doc** file on the companion diskette as a starting point for developing your own portfolio.

Goals

Your goals set a direction for your career and are general in nature. The goals in your portfolio should focus on the professional achievements, skills, and knowledge you want to acquire over the next several years. Companies use these goals to anticipate your developmental needs and interests. They also show management and recruiters that you do indeed have a plan for your future.

Here again, a friend can help you develop your goals. He or she can ask questions that make you think about your goals and can help make sure your goals make sense.

Making Your Goals Work

- **Plan your goals for two to five years from now**—When writing goals, think ahead several years. What do you want to be doing in two years? What do you want to have accomplished four years from today? Goals written for one year or less are often too narrow in focus, and usually concentrate on learning a new position rather than planning for the future. You should also make sure your goals are not so specific as to imply only a narrow interest in the industry or in a specific job. If you are starting in an entry-level position, think about the job you want to be doing in two to three years. Goals can help share your vision for where you will fit in the organization in the future.

- **Make your goals measurable**—Your goals should be specific enough that you will know when you've achieved them. We measure goals in terms of time, money, and resources.

  Too broad:
  "To expand my technical knowledge."

  Good:
  "To develop my database skills by attending a class on Microsoft Access by May 2001."

- **Goals are different from career objectives**—Career objectives are broad and set a direction for your career. Goals are more specific; they include shorter-range objectives that are measurable.

- **Write three to five goals**—If you only write one or two goals, you may appear unfocused and give the impression you're not really interested in advancing your career.

- **Don't make your goals too personal**—Goals such as losing weight or winning a marathon can alienate your interviewer; it may give the person more information than he/she may want to know about sensitive topics. Keep your goals professional and related to your career.

Here is a sample of goals that are appropriate for individuals just starting their careers:

Two-Year Goals

- To hold a leadership role in my department
- To hold at least one active professional membership
- To further develop my computer application skills as they apply to controlling costs
- To earn the customer service award
- To apply my creativity to develop new menus.

Template

Use the **Work Philosophy and Goals.doc** file on the companion diskette as a starting point for developing your own goals and your philosophy.

Your Career Plan

OK... by now you have already dealt with your work philosophy and flushed out at least a couple of years' worth of goals. What happens next? You have spent your time on the "big picture"—NOW you need an action plan. The first step is to take an in-depth look at your skills, interests, and abilities from the professional and personal perspective. Understanding and identifying the different skills you have can help you be better prepared for a job or keep you on track for a promotion. Knowing what you have to offer an employer is important, and you may have more going for you than you think! Once you know where you're going, you can use some techniques to help you develop your action plan.

Identifying Your Skills

When you're in school you are constantly learning new skills. At the beginning of every new class, your teachers usually start by reviewing the goals and objectives for the class. You know what you will be learning and what skills you should have by the time you finish the class. Whether you're taking an accounting class or psychology, you are gaining skills in that area. Skills are often broken down by the type of skill you are learning. **Hard skills** relate to practical skills, like working with computers or operating equipment and machinery. When you follow steps to complete a task, whether it's operating a forklift, keyboarding a report, doing an experiment to produce a reaction, or maintaining an engine on a car, you are doing a hard skill. Most classes are geared to learning a set of hard skills.

Soft skills consist of a broader range of skills related to your personality and attitudes. Examples of soft skills include self-confidence, communication skills, teamwork skills, tolerance, discipline, management, etc. Working on a team project, problem solving a process, leading a meeting, and being able to make decisions are some of the soft skills you can gain from a class without knowing it. They are often thought of as hidden skills, but they are some of the most important skills you can have. Employers are always looking for people with a certain set of hard skills, but when they have good soft skills to go with them, they can be a powerful combination in a good employee. Take a look at the following list to see just what kinds of skills employers are looking for. You can use your portfolio to promote many of these soft skills.

Soft Skills Employers Look For

Teamwork

Being a good team member means:

- Putting the good of the team ahead of yourself
- Respecting others' opinions
- Hearing people out
- Involving everyone in finding solutions to problems.

Presentation skills

- Leading a meeting
- Promoting an idea to the boss
- Giving your thoughts in a union meeting.

Communication skills

- Answering the phone
- Writing e-mails
- Putting together a proposal
- Interacting with co-workers and customers
- Being a good listener
- Giving and receiving feedback.

Attitude

- Enthusiastic, high energy
- Flexible, open-minded
- Dependable.

Leadership

- Heading up a project
- Training others
- Delegating
- Negotiating
- Managing conflict
- Planning
- Setting priorities
- Organizing skills.

Other Soft Skills

- Problem solving
- Multi-tasking
- Thinking quickly
- Ability to make decisions
- Customer service
- Courtesy
- Ability to work with people from different cultures
- Work ethic
- Self-discipline.

Ask the Expert

Identifying the skills I need

Q. **How do I know what skills I need to prove?**

A. A good way to identify what skills you may need to prove is by reviewing job postings for the entry-level position and future positions you may seek. Most potential employers will indicate what skills they value in their job advertisement or job description. Usually, after reviewing a variety of job postings, you will see a pattern of skills desired by potential employers.

Transferable Skills

Transferable skills are the skills you've gathered through various jobs, volunteer work, hobbies, sports, or other life experiences that can be used in your next job or new career. Transferable skills are important to those who are facing a layoff or looking for a different job, new graduates who are looking for their first jobs, and those re-entering the work force after an extended absence. Transferable skills are skills you can use in a variety of industries and settings. A person with management skills can transition from a career in banking to a career in insurance. Good computer skills can be used to develop spreadsheets for a restaurant or track medical records in an office. Begin to identify your skills and how they can be used in different ways. What else can you bring to the table in terms of expertise? Are you a subject matter expert in any fields? The ability to speak a second language could be the asset that sets you apart from other candidates and gets you the job.

Transferable skills can be hard or soft skills. If you can drive a semi truck, a hard skill, you can also drive a delivery van. If you can coach a softball team, you have soft skills that can be used when training people on the job. Take a look at the following list of transferable skills that employers like to see. Notice how many of the skills listed are soft skills. Check out Chapter 9, Resource Guide, for a detailed list of transferable skills.

Transferable Skills

Verbal communication	Leadership
Nonverbal communication	Management
Plan and organize	Financial
Counsel and serve	Administrative
Create and innovate	Analyze
Written communication	Construct and operate
Train/consult	Research
Interpersonal relations	

Strengths, Weaknesses, Opportunities, and Threats to Your Career (SWOT)

A SWOT analysis is a method of looking at the **S**trengths, **W**eaknesses, **O**pportunities, and **T**hreats in a specific situation. In this case, we are applying the process to your career. Strengths and weaknesses are personal to you, they are things you can control. One person may list computer skills as a strength, yet another person may list it as a weakness to their career. How skilled you are is something you can control because you can choose to focus on those skills or you can decide to take a class to improve your skills.

Opportunities and threats are things in your environment that you can't control. Opportunities are positive things that work to your advantage, whereas threats are negative factors that could be a potential setback to your plans. A person considering medical school might list the high salary and prestige of being a doctor as an opportunity, whereas the cost of medical school and the length of time needed to obtain a degree could be listed as a threat. The salary of a doctor and the cost of medical school are things you can't control.

The SWOT analysis is the part of the process where you really size up what you have to offer. When doing a SWOT, you should look at all the characteristics that influence your professional and personal life. Take a look at this shopping list of characteristics for things you **can control** and record your answers on the templates on pages 30 and 31:

- Skills in your field
- Supervision/Management/Leadership abilities
- Types of teams
- Communication (written, electronic, verbal, and non-verbal)
- Technology (types of software and projects)
- Social (professional and service groups)
- Personal areas such as community service.

Give some additional consideration in your analysis to those things you **do not control**:

- Economy/demand for jobs
- Social trends (health, transportation, and e-commerce)
- Political (government or workplace)
- Technology (software and hardware changes)
- Advancement availability (career path, age and experience of those around you)
- Location (job, geography)
- Workplace culture (work ethic, family values, and uses of power)
- Required education (certifications, etc.).

SWOT started as a way to analyze nonprofit organizations and has, in the last 30 years, transitioned to business planning as well as personal planning. You can use a SWOT analysis to help explore issues, skills, strengths, and weaknesses you have in your career search. Look at your skills and abilities in your personal and professional life. Where are you now? What are your strengths? What are your weaknesses? List them under the major headings; then rank them from the strongest to the weakest. Once you know your strengths and weaknesses, you will know what areas to promote and can formulate your goals for where you would like to be.

SWOT Analysis—Your Career

Things You Control

Rank	Your STRENGTHS	Your WEAKNESSES	Rank
	Skills related to your field	Skills related to your field	
	Management	Management	
	Teamwork	Teamwork	
	Communication	Communication	
	Technology - (software, Internet telecommunications, etc.)	Technology - (software, Internet telecommunications, etc.)	
	Social	Social	
	Personal Areas - Family/Friends/ Spiritual/Financial/Health	Personal Areas - Family/Friends/ Spiritual/Financial/Health	

Look at your skills and abilities in your personal and professional life. Where are you now? What are your strengths? What are your weaknesses? List them under the major headings; then rank them from the strongest to the weakest. Once you know your strengths and weaknesses, you will know what areas to promote and can formulate your goals for where you would like to be.

SWOT Analysis—Your Career

Things You Don't Control

Rank	OPPORTUNITIES you can use	THREATS that face you	Rank
	Economy/Demand for Jobs	Economy/Demand for Jobs	
	Social Trends	Social Trends	
	Political (government or workplace)	Political (government or workplace)	
	Techonology	Techonology	
	Advancement Availability	Advancement Availability	
	Location (job, geography)	Location (job, geography)	
	Workplace Culture	Workplace Culture	
	Required Education	Required Education	

Look at the factors above and list the items that have an impact on your career. Look at the career you want. What is the education that you need? Can you get a job anywhere or only in a certain part of the country? Do you want to work in an office environment or can't you stand the thought of being tied down all day? Is the industry you are aiming for in a growth spurt, or are there too many qualified people now? These are all factors that you can't control which will influence your career. Rank them from highest impact to lowest. Knowledge of these issues can help you make better decisions.

 Template

The Career SWOT sheets shown on the previous two pages are available on the companion diskette **(SWOT Analysis.doc)**.

Ask the Expert

I want to be management

Q. **I am currently employed in an hourly position but have goals to get into management as quickly as possible. What can I be doing now to be considered for a management position within my company when the position becomes available?**

A. Begin by gathering evidence of your managerial abilities. Perhaps you have had a job in the past where you were responsible for management type functions, or your current manager has asked you to perform some of his or her managerial duties. What work samples would you have from these experiences?

Consider developing a career portfolio and focusing one entire tabbed section to management work samples and letters of support. Start gathering letters from superiors that attest to your management abilities. When you write your work philosophy, place a heavy emphasis on management and write your goals to indicate a future management direction.

Time to Tell Your Story

Storyboarding is that process in which you "draw mental pictures" of all aspects of your story. Consider storyboarding as a strategic planning tool. Storyboarding is a way to manage the big picture and develop details. Storyboarding got its start with the great Walt Disney who created the process to lay out the animated movies and to carry multiple storylines. This is where you map out your skills and abilities—your story.

How to Storyboard:

- Get yourself a large sheet of paper and sticky notes or a big board.

- Write your goal statements across the top of the paper to serve as categories for organizing skills.
- Work through the questions listed below, putting each answer on a separate sticky note. Concentrate on skills and keywords.
- Post the sticky notes into the goal categories.
- Make a note or map out the work samples you have or need to seek out.
- Take a picture of your map or copy down all your notes and then create your portfolio.

Storyboarding works by allowing you to make multiple lists and to develop and link ideas. A good way to begin is to answer these questions:

- What skills are needed in the position I am working to secure or advance in?
- What skills do I have?
- What am I good at?
- How can I use my current skills in my work?
- What projects have I worked on in school or on the job?
- What do other people think I'm good at?

Use storyboarding to help map out your career.

Building Your Portfolio Plan

Take a look at all the skills you have and the results of your SWOT or storyboard process and build your portfolio plan. It is critical to your success to understand what you have as skills and characteristics, and to create a vision for what you want to do in your profession.

Taking time to evaluate your career and focus your goals will help you in the next phase of the portfolio—putting your résumé together and finding and gathering the proof of your abilities. Don't underestimate the importance of the activities in this chapter. Having the focus will help you determine how to build skill sections of your portfolio and help you focus on producing a valuable tool.

Chapter 3

The Résumé: An Overview of Your Portfolio

Everyone knows about résumés. They are the most common vehicle used in the job-hunting process and are used to convey information about your experiences and qualifications. A résumé usually contains a summary of your education, work experiences, and qualifications for a position. When used in conjunction with your portfolio, the résumé serves as a spring-board for introducing your portfolio into the conversation. It also provides a summary of the contents of the portfolio.

This chapter gives general suggestions for creating your résumé. If you want specific details, you'll find a wealth of information on the Internet. At the end of this chapter, we've included some good websites to help guide you in the process of creating your résumé and making it look its best.

What Goes into Your Résumé?

Creating a résumé is often a daunting task for anyone about to pursue a job search. It is the crucial tool needed to get an interview, and creating it can be a painful experience. There is so much conflicting information about résumés available today. Here are some of the most common questions people ask: "Can it be more than one page?" "Does my education or experience go first?" "What do I do about gaps in my experience?" "How do I make myself look really good without bragging?" "How do I make them see my résumé in the huge pile on the secretary's desk?" "How far back should I go with my experience?" "What if I'm switching fields?" "What if I don't have all the qualifications they are looking for?"

Résumé Basics

If you are just entering the work force, your résumé will look very different from that of a person who has had several years of experience in his or her field. In general, most résumés have a combination of the following sections:

Career Objective/Career Summary—A **career objective** is an overview of the kind of work you want to do: a one- or two-sentence summary of your career goals. If you have been in the workforce for several years, you may want to use a career summary. The **career summary** consists of two to three sentences which briefly outline your career history.

Education—Include any formal education, degrees obtained and in progress, the institution, dates attended, and the focus of your degree(s).

- The less experience you have, the more you need to build up your education. You might consider listing classes you took which are relevant to the field you are entering.
- List any formal education or training programs you have taken which relate to your field.
- List your most recent achievements first.

Work Experience or Skills—Include your job title, name of the organization, dates employed, and an overview of your skills and experience.

- If your work experience is stronger and/or more recent than your education, list your work experience first.
- List your accomplishments and/or responsibilities with each position.
- List your most recent experience first.

Professional Memberships and Services, Awards Received—Include memberships and awards that demonstrate your abilities, enhance your leadership, or document your skills.

Community Service—List organizations and your involvement with them.

Contact Information—Include your name, address, phone number, fax number, e-mail address.

Let Them Know You Have a Portfolio—Your résumé also needs a line at the bottom of the last page indicating that your portfolio is available for review:

Career Portfolio and References available for review

Organizing Your Résumé

There are several standard ways of organizing a résumé depending on your experiences, skills, and target industry:

- **Chronological Résumés**—Information is organized by date. Information is listed in order of time elapsed, with the most recent experiences first. This is the most common and straightforward résumé format.

- **Functional Résumés**—This type of résumé is designed to highlight accomplishments and specific skills. It is organized by the different kinds of skills you can perform, such as management skills, marketing, finance, etc.

- **Performance Résumés**—This résumé type is a combination of the chronological and functional approaches. You list employment information in a chronological format, then organize the skills you've developed in each position in order to highlight your accomplishments.

- **Focused Résumés**—This is a tailor-made résumé designed for specific professions such as teachers, civil servants, computer professionals, lodging professionals, food service operators, etc. This résumé only lists those jobs you've had which directly relate to the specific area you are targeting. This format is often used by large corporations to track performance and skills within their own organization. If you are looking for promotion within a company, this format may suit your needs. This format is not as popular because it is very specific.

- **Government Résumés**—If you are interviewing for a government position or with a company that contracts with the government, you may be asked to submit a standardized résumé, laid out in a specific format. They are usually narrative in nature, and should use terms from standardized job descriptions and other government documents.

Ask the Expert

Résumé Do's and Don'ts

Q. **How do I choose which organizational style to use?**

A. It depends on your audience and your experience. People with limited experience and education should use the chronological layout. If you have more experience and/or education and want to emphasize your skills or course work, use a performance résumé. That way you can list your courses and highlight skills obtained from your jobs. If you have been in the work force for several years, and are looking to highlight your skills for a promotion or applying for a job where you are emphasizing your experience, use the functional résumé.

Q. **What if I am short on education or work experience?**

A. If you are coming out of college and looking for a starting position, you'll want to emphasize your course work. Highlight the classes that related to your major and indicate the types of skills you gained from the courses. Use any community service or volunteer work you have done that may show leadership, experience, or skills. Join a professional organization that will get you connected to other people in your industry. Get teachers or others who have experienced your work to write you a letter of recommendation, highlighting what you have done.

Q. **Do I put education or work experience first?**

A. If you have education but limited work experience, list education first. If you have been in the work force for several years, list experience first. If you are changing fields and your work experience doesn't relate to the area you are entering, list experience first, highlighting your transferable skills. You decide which is stronger: your education or your work experience.

Q. **Do I list everything I've done?**

A. If you have limited work experience, list it all. If you have had a variety of short-term positions, list the jobs that are relevant to the position you are applying for. Some experts recommend leaving off any experiences older than 10 years, but if the experiences have value and add to your employability in the current position, go ahead and list them.

Q. **What do I do if I have time gaps in my résumé?**

A. If you're talking about timelines where you were unemployed for a period of time, leave the gap and be prepared to talk about it if the question arises in an interview.

Q. **What do I do if I have skill gaps in my résumé?**

A. If you have skill gaps, where you don't have all of the qualifications for the position but you are applying anyway, you will want to emphasize your strengths and your ability to learn new skills. The cover letter that goes with the résumé may be the best place to address this. Be sure to use keywords specific to the industry so your résumé will have a better chance of getting to the "interview" pile.

Q. **What if I don't have any awards or memberships?**

A. It's okay if you don't have awards or professional memberships. You can use your work experience and education to promote your abilities. It is a good idea to join a professional organization in your field in order to keep learning and growing professionally. Many organizations have student branches for professionals just entering the field. Join the organizations that will help you continue to learn new things and grow.

Q. **Should I list my references on the résumé?**

A. Most employers do not contact references until you have been interviewed and you are being considered for the position. Besides, you may need all that room to list skills gained from course work or job experiences. Create a separate reference sheet and indicate on your résumé that your Career Portfolio and References are available upon request. Include a copy of the references in your portfolio and keep an individual copy available to give to the interviewer if it is requested.

Q. **I've heard that my résumé should fit on one page. Can I go over one page in length?**

A. As a general rule, if you are just out of school, you should be able to keep your résumé to one page. If you have more experience you can expand it. Even the most experienced person should keep his or her résumé to three pages. Your résumé can be longer than one page, but be sure the information you include is a good representation of you. Some experts say you should always fill the extra pages. Don't have a one and a half page résumé. Today, more résumés are being sorted and processed electronically, where a computer program scans for certain keywords. You may benefit from listing key skills and abilities you have gained from your experiences, and that can take up more space.

Q. **Can I use a fancy type style and paper to help my résumé stand out from the rest?**

A. With many job openings generating hundreds of applications, employers are looking to technology to help them deal with the volume of applicants. They will often scan a résumé into electronic format and then use a software program to scan for certain keywords in the résumé. One of the problems with fancy type styles is that they don't scan well. The software is used to dealing with plain type styles and can mess up on fancy ones. The last thing you want is to have your résumé scanned and your name come in wrong because you have it in a funky font. The same rule goes for paper. Using paper with shaded or mottled backgrounds can cause the scanner to misread words.

Your best option is to use a readable font, on high quality white paper. Lay out your résumé with plenty of white space in an attractive format and use appropriate keywords to set your résumé apart. Check out Chapter 8, Style Guide, for more details on making your résumé look great.

 Template

Most word processing programs such as Microsoft Word and Word Perfect include templates for creating résumés. We suggest you use these templates as a starting point for creating your own résumé.

Choosing the Right Words

Regardless of the style of résumé you choose to create, you should describe the skills and experiences associated with your jobs and education. Using the right words to capture experience can sometimes be challenging. When it comes to identifying skills and items for the résumé and the career portfolio, you'll want to use a combination of action verbs and keywords. The technology of today has shifted people's thinking—while they are still looking for action-oriented people (action verbs), they are also looking for ways to quickly dial into who and what you are by descriptive things you can do. What concrete terms can be used to describe you? Focus on the skills and keyword terms that are core to your specific profession.

Add Keywords to Your Résumé

"Keywords" are those terms that cue people in to specific skills and abilities. If you've ever used a search engine on the Internet, you've used keywords. Think about your résumé as if it were a website. What terms do you want people to look for and find? A person wanting to be employed in the technology field might list the software packages he/she works in. Also include business functions such as "web design" or "meeting planning," etc. Employers use keywords to screen applicants for interviews. Make sure your résumé makes the cut.

Action verbs are used on a résumé to describe what you have done. Here are a few action verbs to get you thinking:

accomplished, advised, assessed, authorized, budgeted, completed, conducted, demonstrated, managed, encouraged, maintained, recommended, scheduled, solved, etc..

A more extensive list of action verbs is included in Chapter 9, Resource Guide, for use in your résumé to indicate the action you have completed. Use them with keywords to demonstrate your skills. As a rule, scanned résumés look more at keywords, whereas a résumé reviewed by a person tends to note the action verbs. In the following descriptions the **action verb is in bold** and the keywords are underlined:

- **Managed** a team of four documentation writers
- **Maintained** a database of 25,000 customers
- Meeting planning - Helped **plan, organize,** and **manage** the 2001, 2002, and 2003 Midwest CHRIE conferences - Committee member
- Webmaster - **designed** website, **maintained** online registration, **managed** conference database and registration

The Scannable Résumé

With the volume of applicants for positions, more companies are using computers to select potential candidates for the interview process. The software and scanning technology is quite advanced, and it is more cost effective than paying an employee to do the same work. With the thought in mind that your résumé may never be read by a real person, it's time to plan ahead and create a résumé that appeals to both the computer and the human reader. You can do this by using keywords and action verbs and by formatting the résumé in a way that can be scanned easily by a computer. Here are some guidelines for making your résumé scanner friendly:

- Use black ink on 8 1/2" x 11" white paper, printed only on one side.
- Don't use italic or underline.
- Use 12- to 14-pitch font size for body text and 16- to 18-pitch fonts for headings.
- Use a non-decorative type style.
- Place your name on each page in the header or footer.
- Use one-inch margins all the way around the document. (During the scanning process, margins are sometimes trimmed and information could be lost with a smaller margin.)
- Avoid using staples or folding the résumé on a line of text.
- Avoid the use of graphics, shading, and lines.
- Identify dates and times you are available at different contact addresses. Include e-mail addresses where possible.
- Use keywords—Using the vocabulary and terminology of your industry is critical. Using terms like "dollar volume," "number of people supervised," "franchise vs. corporate owned," etc., may allow your résumé to be selected over another.

Here is a scannable performance résumé with good use of
action verbs and keywords:

Shauna R. Johnson

711 Oak Street • Conner, Indiana • 47331 • Phone: 825.765.7222 • E-mail: shauy@si-net.com

Objective	Design, develop, and implement instructional programs in an adult educational setting

Summary of Skills

Communications	*Leadership*	*Computer*
Oral Presentations	Training	Windows 95 and 98
Reports	Customer Service	MS Word
Business Letters	Ordering	MS Publisher
Copy Writing	Scheduling	Page Maker
Proof Reading	Merchandising	Freehand
Editing	Displays	E-Mail
Page Layout	Management Skills	Web Navigation
Document Design	Organizational Skills	Desk Top Publishing
Interpersonal Skills	Conflict and Group Management	

Education

Expected Graduation Date • May 2000 • Indiana University East • Richmond, Indiana
BA • General Studies
> Concentration in Psychology
> Specialty in Tourism Management
>> Certificate Safe Serve Food Service Sanitation
>> Certificate Tourism Management with courses in:
Management
Marketing
Human Resource Management
Tourism
Hospitality
Sanitation

Awards

Consistently Named to the Dean's List
1997 and 1999 Nominee Student of the Year
1999 General Studies Distinguished Student
Other Awards Appear in Portfolio

Professional Experience

1997—Present   Indiana University East   Richmond, Indiana
Hospitality/Tourism Management Program Assistant • Writing Lab Tutor • Peer Mentor
Connersville Center Associate • Orientation Coordinator

> Instructing, and Tutoring Students in the Art of Note-taking, Learning Styles, Organizational Skills, Scheduling, and Other Academic Areas
> Organizing, Coordinating, and Implementing New Student Orientations
> Reviewing and Editing Student Compositions
> Reviewing Student Assignments and Portfolios
> Advising New and Returning Students in the Areas of University Resources, Scheduling, and Prerequisite Courses, and Retention Issues
> Marketing and Recruiting

Collegiate Activities

1997-Present • President • Alpha Sigma Lambda Honor Society • Theta Mu Chapter
1996-Present • President • Pacesetters and Activities Council of Connersville

Community Activities

1996-1998 • Chapter Leader • Indiana Chronic Fatigue Syndrome Association • Connersville
Regular Election Poll Worker • Sheriff
Sunday School Teacher

Portfolio

Available for review

*This professional résumé includes a summary of skills organized by area. It
also integrates keywords and action verbs to describe work experiences.*

New Trends in Résumés

Online Résumé Services

These days you may end up finding a job by placing your résumé in an electronic database. A growing number of services will scan your résumé and place it on the Internet or other database services. Many of these websites are geared to people in certain industries. Such sites are popular with employers because they can get the résumés of prospective employees who are already screened to a certain industry.

Some services will scan your résumé and ask you to complete a brief application, including items such as salary preferences, employers, willingness to travel, distance willing to travel, etc. The service gives employers access to "at a glance" peeks at your résumé. For a fee, they will give an employer a copy of the entire résumé via fax. After that, it's up to the employer to contact you.

Some of these services will provide you with feedback on who requested your résumé and the salary ranges other professionals with similar skills are earning in the industry. They will also identify trends in professional fields, such as a need for increased computer skills for Restaurant Management.

Professional databases are available not only to college graduates, but also to professionals trying to determine the marketability of their skills. You can find these databases by browsing on the Internet using key terms such as **career placement**, **job search**, and **employment**. Within the databases, you can search for openings by experience, salary ranges, key interest areas, etc. For using these services you will sometimes pay a flat fee of $25 to $75. In other cases, your résumé is scanned for free and the employer pays for access.

College Placement Websites

Many colleges and university placement centers have embraced the Internet and are using it to the advantage of graduates and alumni alike. Many schools keep a résumé database, whereas others are providing students with space for personal web pages. If you have the opportunity to create your own website, check out Chapter 6, The Electronic Portfolio, for tips and guidelines for creating your site.

Web Page Résumés

More people are now putting résumés online with their own web pages. The really savvy people are creating more than just résumés—they're creating online portfolios. It's especially critical that your résumé be well developed so you can gain the attention of the person searching your page. Links and key terms are critical. See Chapter 6, The Electronic Portfolio, for more details.

Sending Out Your Résumé

Keep in mind that your résumé is the tool that gets you an interview. Your résumé needs to represent you and should be a professional looking document. Be sure to double and triple check your résumé for typos, formatting errors, and correct information. Simple errors can show a lack of attention to details and may cause your résumé to be automatically rejected by some employers.

Cover Letters

A cover letter is sent with the résumé and should briefly explain what sets you apart from others and why you would be the best person for the job. Employers use the cover letter to check for writing style, attention to detail and tone, as well as your qualifications. Here are a few "do's" for cover letters:

- Check your spelling and grammar
- Address the letter to the specific person who will be reviewing your letter
- Draw attention to key summaries of your résumé
- Explain what types of opportunities you are looking to secure.

E-Mailing Your Résumé

Occasionally you may be asked to e-mail your résumé to a prospective employer or contact at an organization. This is often the case when you have a personal contact with someone in the organization. E-mailing your résumé gives you quick strike ability. You can react faster and have your résumé on the employer's desk faster than with regular mail. Here are some general guidelines to follow when e-mailing a résumé:

- **Send your résumé as an attachment**—Send the résumé as a Word file or an Adobe PDF (Portable Document File) so it can be printed out by the receiver.

- **Include a cover letter**—Send the cover letter as an attachment, or write your cover letter in the body of the e-mail.

- **Include your contact information in the body of the e-mail**—This way if there are any problems with the files, the receiver can get to you as quickly as possible.

- **Save your résumé in a PDF format if possible**—The recipient must have a program called Acrobat Viewer on their computer. The program can be downloaded from the Internet for free. This format can be printed directly from the browser, and the document also cannot be edited or changed by anyone else. Check your computer center or Placement Office for assistance on creating PDFs.

- **Use standard fonts like Times New Roman or Arial when sending your résumé document**—If the receiver's computer doesn't have your funky font installed, your document will print with different fonts and will not look its best.

- **Use your private e-mail, not a corporate account**—Organizations have the right to monitor their employees' e-mail. If you are currently employed and looking for another job, you should correspond through a private e-mail account, not the corporate address. You probably don't want your current employer to know you're actively looking for a new job.

- **Send a hard copy of your résumé and cover letter by mail**—Follow up your e-mail with a hard copy to reinforce your e-mail message and to serve as a backup copy.

Faxing Your Résumé

You can also respond quickly to a request by faxing your résumé to an employer. Since the quality of a fax machine copy is inferior to a printed hard copy, you should send this only at the request of the organization. Here are a few guidelines to consider when faxing a résumé:

- **Fax from a copy of your résumé printed on white paper**—Colored paper and paper with texture do not fax well and tend to be grainy and hard to read. White paper will fax better.

- **Include a cover letter**—Send the cover letter and résumé together with a cover sheet directed to the correct person.

- **Use standard fonts like Times New Roman or Arial when sending your résumé**—Again, funky fonts don't always print well on the other end of the fax machine.

- **Consider the uses of your office fax machine**—The sending fax machine produces a log of all faxes sent. It often lists the name of the organization at the receiving end of a fax. Consider carefully if you want your employer to know you're faxing things to another organization or competitor.

- **Make sure the fax goes through**—Be sure you stand at the machine until the fax has been successfully sent. If it doesn't go through or the line is busy it may drop your fax job. Wait for a confirmation statement from the fax machine.

- **Send a hard copy of your résumé and cover letter by mail**—Follow up your fax with a hard copy to reinforce your message and to serve as a backup copy.

Your Résumé Sets the Stage

In Chapter 2 you planned out your portfolio and decided where to focus your efforts. By developing your résumé, you have identified the educational and job-related experiences you want to emphasize. You have really created an overview of your portfolio, the first step to creating the finished product. Use your résumé as a guide in the next two chapters as you begin to collect and organize work samples. As you begin to sort and decide on work samples, you may find that your résumé needs to be adjusted. Congratulations! You're on your way to creating a focused portfolio that will help provide backup and support to your résumé!

Related Websites

Here are just a few of the thousands of websites designed to help you create the perfect résumé. Use these sites as guidelines. Remember, you are creating a product that represents **you** to potential employers. Follow your instincts and create the résumé that feels right to you.

- **America's Job Bank** - http://www.ajb.dni.us/
- **America's Talent Bank** - http://atb.mesc.state.mi.us/
- **CareerCity** - http://www.careercity.com/
- **CareerMagazine** - http://www.careermag.com/
- **CareerMosaic** - http://www.careermosaic.com/
- **CareerPath.com** - http://www.careerpath.com/
- **CareerWeb** - http://www.careerweb.com/
- **JobBank USA** : Jobs MetaSEARCH - http://www.jobbankusa.com/search.html/
- **JobTrak** - http://www.jobtrak.com/
- **Online Career Center** - http://www.occ.com/
- **Resumail** - http://www.resumail.com/
- **ResumeBlaster** - http://www.resumeblaster.com/
- **The Job Hunters Bible** - What Color Is My Parachute? - http://www.jobhuntersbible.com/
- **The Monster Board** - http://www.monster.com/
- **Weddle's Web Guide** - http://www.nbew.com/
- **The Career Clinic** - http://www.thecareerclinic.com/

CHAPTER **4**

PROVING YOUR SKILLS

This chapter is all about proof. Chapters 2 and 3 helped determine what skill areas you need to emphasize. Now we'll take that information and look at how to find, create, and select work samples, certificates, letters of recommendation, skill sets, and support materials which make up the heart of your portfolio. In this chapter you'll find the details on:

- Finding and choosing work samples
- Asking for and using letters of recommendation
- Creating works in progress
- Working with skill sets
- Using certifications, diplomas, degrees, and awards
- Using community service to prove your skills
- Using academic plan of study and faculty/employer bios
- Creating the reference materials needed to support your portfolio.

Look at the Big Picture

Decide what skill areas you want to emphasize, whether it's Communications, Management, Accounting, Restaurant Management, Computer Skills, Graphics, Menu Development, Leadership, Auditing, or Public Relations. Try to have three to five different areas. Then select work samples that correspond to these areas. If you don't have very many work samples, you may find yourself creating categories to support your samples. It's important to make sure the samples you use support your goals and will show your best work.

Work Samples

Work samples make up the major portion of the portfolio and become the most powerful part of your sales pitch.

Work samples are proof of your knowledge and skills. When assembling your portfolio for an interview, you can customize your work samples to match the skills needed for the position. You can "wow" a potential employer by showing examples that clearly demonstrate skills he or she wants to see. Work samples also add to your credibility. Instead of just telling someone what you have done, you can show examples.

Sources of Work Samples

Common sources for work samples include:

- Classroom projects from your major core courses during school
- Materials you have generated while on the job or on an internship or co-op
- Materials completed in community service projects or professional memberships.

Class Assignments

Projects you developed to fulfill course requirements are a great source of work samples. The grade you earned on the project is usually not included, but could be brought up as a point of discussion in the interview. Some examples include:

- Real-life simulations
- A feasibility study you generated in a marketing class
- The menu you designed for your menu design project or capstone food course
- A business plan you developed
- An advertising campaign you developed as a team effort
- Office or facility designs.

Anything you create that shows your skill in a particular area can be used as a work sample. If the physical evidence is too big to fit in the portfolio (like a poster or diagram) take a picture of the item and include the photo.

The more details you can give about the project, the better. You may want to include some of the following items for each project sample:

- The faculty assignment sheet—you may have to rekey it so that it is presentable
- Table of contents for the entire project
- Names of people working on the project
- Assignment summaries
- Why it was generated, the purpose it served
- Executive summaries where possible
- Financial summaries where appropriate
- Pictures
- Multimedia summaries
- What you learned from the project
- Any prerequisites to this assignment.

Ask the Expert -

I got rid of all my projects...

Q. **I'm a senior—I did a lot of projects, but I've thrown them out. What can I put in my portfolio to show my experiences?**

A. It's always frustrating when you realize you had great projects that would show experience but you've cleared your "clutter" and thrown them away. Check and see if your instructor has an assignment sheet for the project which could be included in the portfolio. You could also write up a project summary; list the assignment, what you created, and what you learned from it. Keep the project summary sheet to a single page. Depending on the type of project, you may also have photos that could be used.

On-the-Job Samples, Co-Op Projects, or Internship Projects

Having a hard time coming up with work samples? Take a look at the things you do on the job and consider the things you create and work with on a daily basis that show your experience. Consider these work sample ideas:

- Sections of the employee handbook
- Departmental operating procedures
- Programs or systems created
- Campaigns created or advanced
- Market research techniques
- Promotional materials
- Job projects such as employee newsletters
- Special events created
- Multimedia presentations created.

 Ask the Expert

I need some experience!

Q. **I recently obtained my diploma and graduated with honors, but in my field there aren't many jobs open. Those that are advertising want someone with experience. So far, I have my résumé posted on several job search web sites, but that hasn't been too productive either. Any advice?**

A. It seems you have a lot to offer. There are a couple of ways to address the work experience problem:

1. Seek out a paid internship with a respected company. Go in with an educational contract where you want to have specific work experience to document. You need at least six months experience and often this can be worked around another position as long as you are up front as to what you want to accomplish.

2. Find any class projects you generated which could serve as work samples in your career portfolio.

3. You need to be prepared for more than just the obvious fields where you can use your skills. Determine your transferable skills and find out other industries that need people with these skills. The hospitality, lodging, and restaurant management industry is a field where people from many different backgrounds can apply their skills. Broaden your search. Consider joining a professional association where you can network and become known—it adds to your credibility while you build work experience.

Community Service Projects

Community involvement is a great source of work samples often overlooked by people as they pull together their portfolios. Service samples may be written projects or pictures of your involvement in community service. Examples include:

- The poster and picture of the "Brotherhood Tree of Giving" you designed for the lobby of a hotel
- The grant proposal you helped create for a day-care facility
- A flyer you created for the June mailing
- A picture of your team building a house
- A photo of you working in a soup kitchen
- The menu you developed for the PTA dinner
- The menu and production plan for a catered dinner for 80.

Include the following information for each community service sample:

- A summary sheet of what you accomplished
- Results of the project
- Who helped you
- A photo if appropriate.

If your community service samples relate to one of your skill areas, you may choose to put your sample there. If your service experience doesn't relate, you should create a separate tabbed section for community service.

 Bright Idea!

Employers like to see community service involvement. Use your volunteerism to demonstrate your skills.

Your Commitment to Personal Growth

Employers want to know that you are committed to the job and to the company. They also want to see you grow and expand professionally because it's good for business. Having a plan for your own professional development and growth in your field shows your commitment to yourself and your career. Most people achieve professional growth through professional memberships and certifications.

Professional Memberships and Services

Professional memberships and services show your commitment to the field and demonstrate how you will keep up with the growing and changing knowledge/skills in the field. You should be carrying at least one professional membership at all times.

Professional memberships show your desire to grow in your career.

What professional groups should you belong to? You'll find many professional groups outside your company. Join professional organizations related to your area of business rather than those that are merely social organizations. Seeking out leadership roles in a professional organization is one way to demonstrate your management and leadership abilities. Professional memberships are usually listed under a separate tabbed area in your portfolio, and are usually no more than two to four pages in length. You should include the following information:

- **A list of organizations to which you belong**
- **The date you joined**
- **Offices, boards, or committees on which you've served**
- **Appropriate letters of accomplishment**
- **Photographs of events or copies of programs where you have provided a presentation or service.**

- **Provide proof of your membership.** Use a membership card or a letter from the president of the organization as proof of your membership. If your membership card is your canceled check, use the letter instead.
- **Spell out the name of the organization, don't just use its abbreviation.** Listing a membership in the NRA could be referring to the National Restaurant Association or the National Rifle Association.

Sample:

Professional Memberships

- CMA (Club Managers of America)—Member since 2001
- Marketing Committee Chair—2002–Present
- Toastmasters, since 2000.

 Template

Use the template on the enclosed disk to create your own membership listing. **(Memberships.doc)**

Using the Portfolio to Track Certifications and Professional Development

As we said in the first chapter, a portfolio is a great tool for managing information. The portfolio is the perfect place to store all the certificates, checklists, and plans necessary for many certification programs. Depending on your certification process, you may have a structured set of materials that you can put into the portfolio where you can list or mark down what you have accomplished to date. If no formal plan fits, you can create your own forms and lists to track your progress. As you obtain new skills, add them to your portfolio or check them off your list.

Be sure to collect work samples as you complete your certification. Projects, letters of recommendation, and skill sets help document your experience. If you are in the process of completing a certification, make sure one of your career goals is the completion of the certification program.

Keep in mind that certifications and advanced degrees can take a considerable amount of time and effort to complete. Ask yourself some of these questions to determine why you want the degree:

- Does your future career path require a certificate or degree to be qualified?
- Will your salary increase enough to pay for the advanced cost of education over time?
- Do you enjoy learning? Advanced degrees can be more interesting than undergraduate work because they focus on a particular area, but they often require great amounts of timely work.

 Ask the Expert

Do I need certification?

Q. **Entry-level positions in my career field do not require me to hold any certifications. Should I go for any sort of certifications while I am still in college, or wait until I get into the industry?**

A. Certifications can provide a boost to the start of your career. Applicants that show an interest in their career field, be it through certifications or association memberships, or in other ways, can have a real edge over other applicants. Also, having a certification can improve your starting salary.

Be sure to take the time to investigate the certification. Ensure whatever certifications you choose to go after are nationally recognized. A couple good ways to determine what certifications will meet your needs can include:

- Looking on the Internet and the want ads in the local paper
- Reviewing the jobs in your career field and determining what types of certifications they are looking for
- Contacting your career association and determining what types of certifications the members hold.

Memberships and certifications can help prove to an employer that you are serious about your job and your career. Take some time to look at your "master plan" and decide how this can all work together to advance your career. Education is valued, and when packaged correctly, you can open many doors and have fun.

Putting It Together

Work samples are the dynamic portion of your portfolio. As you prepare for different job interviews, your portfolio needs to be adjusted as well. You may need to change the work samples you show to demonstrate specific abilities that are desired by the company. You need to evaluate your portfolio before each interview to make sure it fits the prospective employer's needs. Selecting the correct work samples and keeping them organized for instant access is very important. Follow these guidelines to help you in selecting your samples:

- **How to select the best work samples**—Ask yourself the following questions about each sample:
    - What will this work demonstrate—skills, competencies, or achievement of goals?
    - Is this my best work?
    - Does it show mastery?
    - Am I proud of this sample . . . all or part of it?
- **Include a sample, not the whole project**—Try to limit yourself to a maximum of 20 pages per project. People don't want to read everything.
- **Offer the full project**—Add a line on a work sample overview card offering the full project:

    Full project available upon request

- **Identify people who contributed to the project**—When presenting work samples, clearly identify its purpose and everyone who has contributed to the sample.
- **When in doubt, leave it out**—Never include a work sample that you are not proud to be associated with, now or in the future. Remember that more is not necessarily better; in fact, it could be the "kiss of death."
- **Use a photo summary**—A photo summary of your work may be the best way to relay work experience. Create photos which show summaries of your work, not just the physical

environment. Include pictures of yourself in action with the project.

- **Make it look good**—Select the best way to present your work samples: through text or photos. (See Chapter 8, A Matter of Style, for more information.)

- **Use grouped sheet protectors for projects**—You can purchase special sets of 5 or 10 interconnected sheet protectors. Use these to keep an entire project sample together so you can easily switch out projects in the portfolio when customizing it to the employer.

- **Pay attention to confidentiality**—Materials generated on the job are usually the property of the company you were working for at the time you created the material. When you display or show that material, be sure to recognize the owner. If you have signed a confidentiality agreement with a company, you should not include their work in your portfolio.

It's Confidential...

John included materials from his job in his work samples and indicated on the sample cards that the material was used with permission. He interviewed with his portfolio but didn't get the job. When he asked the interviewer for feedback, the interviewer said he was concerned about how an applicant who used confidential samples in an interview would handle confidentiality on the job.

Keeping Track of Your Work Samples

- **Have a schedule for updating your collection of work samples**—Develop a routine for collecting materials. If you are in school, you may choose midterm and final exam time to stop and consider which, if any, of your projects should be saved for your files. On the job, make a 30- to 60-minute appointment with yourself once every quarter to take time to reflect on your work over the past months. You should consider completed reports, projects, awards, achievements, or project summaries.

- **Keep track of your work samples**—Get a large plastic tote with hanging folders. You should keep original copies of projects, letters of recommendations, letters of accommodation, or certificates of achievement or degrees. You don't need to spend lots of time arranging it; you just need a designated place to keep your materials.

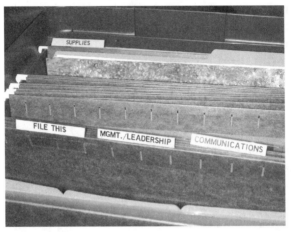

Use a tote with files to store your work samples and supplies.

- **Include the correct work samples**—The work samples you include in your portfolio will vary, based on the needs of the potential employer. You should have a collection of different work samples stored in your tote or filing cabinet. Each sample should be in its own set of sheet protectors, so you can quickly swap out appropriate work samples as needed.

- **Organize work samples into the appropriate skill areas**— Work samples should be clustered by major skill areas. You determine these skill areas. Each skill area will have its own tabbed section in the portfolio. Each skill area should contain work samples that emphasize that particular area. See the section on Skill Sets in this chapter for more information on organizing the skills area section of your portfolio.

- **Organize work samples within a skill area**—The organization and flow of work samples will vary with each sample. Try to break up text and photos so the arrangement creates growing interest and piques curiosity. You may want to organize your work samples in a flow that shows growth or chronological advancement.

- **Use work sample overview cards**—A work sample overview card is a small card containing a brief summary of the work sample. It is placed inside the page protector of the first page of your sample, and helps the reader remember what he or she is looking at and why. We recommend that you create cards for each work sample using a blank sheet of standard size business cards. Format the page on your computer, and include the following information:

  - Title of the project
  - Purpose of the project
  - Date of work
  - Who worked with you
  - What skills are demonstrated using keywords.

Sample:

Marketing Feasibility Study for Franchise Hotel
Fall Term 2003
Group project—Anna Davis, Mark Warner, Karen Kingston, & David Morrow
Analysis—Competitive, customer, SWOT

 Template

Use the template on the enclosed disk to create your own work sample overview cards. **(Work Sample Overview Cards.doc)**

Letters of Recommendation

Letters of recommendation from employers, instructors, etc., can provide additional proof of your abilities. Letters provide personal references from people who have seen you perform. You may need to rely more on letters of recommendation when you don't have many work samples, or when the type of work you do doesn't facilitate written samples.

You should solicit letters from people who know you and/or your work personally. Instructors, supervisors, owners, presidents, and managers—all can be appropriate references. Whoever you choose should be familiar with your work and be able to judge performance and competency. You should be proud to be associated with these people. If you don't like them, they probably don't like you, and you don't want a letter from them.

Asking for a Letter

- You should request your letter of recommendation in writing long before you need it.
- Your letter needs to help guide the person writing the recommendation to focus his or her letter on key skills and areas of your personality that you want addressed.
- Ask for the letter while you are close to the event or you still have an opportunity for contact with the person.
- You should always allow two to three weeks for receiving the letter, as people tend to get busy. It is appropriate to follow up with them a week after your request.

To ask for a recommendation, remember to start with courtesy and manners; say Please and Thank You frequently, and in a heartfelt way. Remember, these people hold your success in the palm of their hands. Your goal, the purpose of a letter, is to document your performance, to have your achievement recognized, and/or to have your abilities summarized. **Most people write lousy letters of recommendation.** They tend to make the letters too general or generic. You need to help the person you choose to write the letter. When writing your letter, begin by telling the person the purpose of the letter: for your portfolio, for graduate school, for an internship, or a press release. Then, dial in your reference by giving them a list of traits, skills, or attributes you want addressed. Here are some examples:

- Leadership
- Ability to work in groups
- Ability to self-motivate
- Ability to meet customer needs
- Ability to complete work
- Ability to supervise
- Management skills
- Creativity
- People skills.

The Perfect Letter

The letter should be on official letterhead, should have an ink signature, and should not be folded. The recommendation letter you receive should be addressed as "Dear Future Employer." Do not use the generic, open-ended salutations such as "To Whom It May Concern" . . . or "Dear Sir or Madame." It should also include background information on how the reference knows you and how long you have been associated with the organization or project. He or she should explain how long you have been associated and in what capacity.

Don't be afraid to proof their work. If you find a mistake, be humble and ask for a correction.

Letters of recommendation will go in one of three places in the portfolio—work sample documentation, professional service/membership, and/or community service. If the letter is comprehensive, discussing two or more of these sections, include it in the work samples and refer to it in the other area. A sample request letter is shown on the next page.

 Template

A sample recommendation request letter is included on the accompanying diskette. Use it as a starting point for writing your own letters. **(Recommendation request.doc)**

Sample Request Letter

Inside Address

Today's date

Dear Professor Brush:

I was a student of yours last term in your Hospitality Senior Seminar class. I earned an A in your class, so you probably remember me. I will be graduating in May, and I am currently working on assembling my career portfolio. Could you please write a letter of recommendation addressing the following skills:

- My ability to work in groups.
- My ability to do presentations.
- My ability to perform academically.
- My ability to do electronic spreadsheets.
- My ability to read an income statement.

It would also be helpful if you could indicate how long you have known me and on what occasions you have worked with me. I would also appreciate it if you could address the letter to "Dear Future Employer."

I would greatly appreciate receiving this letter within the next two weeks. Please call or e-mail me and let me know when it would be convenient for me to pick up the letter. It would be helpful if I could pick up an unfolded letter. Thank you very much for your consideration and all your help. Please feel free to call me if you have any questions.

Sincerely,

David Morrow

David Morrow
123 45th Ave.
Any State, NY 01011
(123)456-7890 - Home phone
e-mail: davidm@provider.com

Transferable Skills

Transferable skills are skills you can use in a variety of industries and settings. A person with management skills can successfully transition from a career in banking to a career in insurance. Good computer skills can be used to develop spreadsheets for a restaurant or track medical records in an office. Begin to identify your skills and how they can be used in different ways. What else can you bring to the table in terms of expertise? Are you a subject matter expert in any fields? The ability to speak a second language could be the asset that sets you apart from other candidates and gets you the job. As our economy becomes more global, many companies are looking to their employees for more than the requirements of the job. Having transferable skills can lead to more opportunities and the ability to transition to different jobs as the market shifts.

 Ask the Expert

I need more work samples!

Q. **I am about to graduate college with a modest grade point average. I will have a BA degree, but I have very limited work experience and have not done any community service. I guess I was never all that focused on my future. Are my class projects the only work samples I can use? Are there any other ways I can prove I have skills?**

A. A great place to look for hidden skills can be in your everyday life. Many times you have "Life Skills" that can be transferred into the workplace. Things such as financial planning, budgeting, time management, organizational skills, and technological skills can all be developed in your everyday life. For example, everyone needs to budget their money in order to have enough to pay bills, for basic needs such as food and shelter, for entertainment, etc. You may budget using a computer program, by a pencil and paper method, or even in your head. Anyway you slice it, it's still budgeting. Consider using a spreadsheet to create your household budget, and use it as a work sample! This can be done for several different skills you develop in your everyday life. Other examples can include:

- A weekly schedule to show time management skills
- Copies of items you have created using various computer programs to show your knowledge and ability with those programs
- The layout of a filing system you have developed to prove organizational skills.

Take a look at the transferable skills list in Chapter 9 for more ideas on marketable skills you might want to include in your portfolio.

Ask the Expert

Using nonacademic activities

Q. **I am involved in a lot of nonacademic activities. Is there anything I should use in my career portfolio?**

A. Yes. Employers respect transferable skills, especially in the area of soft skills or interpersonal skills such as teamwork, presentation skills, leadership, problem solving, and others. Good ways to document these skills are through:

- Letters of referral
- Customer comment letters
- Awards and recognitions received.

Be sure to link the skills you gain from nonacademic activities to the position you are targeting. Use your project overview cards to link the work sample to the skill sets you are trying to demonstrate. Sports, clubs, community service can all serve as excellent sources of skill development. Be sure to collect your work samples now—you can sort them later as you customize your portfolio to your targeted employer.

Works in Progress

This is a place to list projects on which you are currently working. You may choose to show parts or modules that are completed enough to demonstrate a skill, competency, or achievement. This section may be very short. It should be clearly labeled "Works in Progress," and can be placed at the beginning of the work samples. You may want to use a bulleted list. During an interview you may refer to this list of current projects after you have discussed your work samples. It can serve to transition the interviewer or supervisor into more questions. Your list should include:

- The expected completion date
- Whom the work is for
- What skills or competencies it demonstrates.

Skill Sets

What Are Skill Sets?

In some professions, you just may not have a lot of physical work samples available. A listing of your skills and how well you can do them can be used in your portfolio to demonstrate your skills and abilities. A **skill set** is a list of related skills grouped together. The look and feel of a skill set will vary depending on where you got it from. Many organizations and professions have developed skill sets for their particular fields. If you can't find any, you can always create your own skill sets.

Skill sets are not only a list of your abilities, but they also show the level of your abilities. Skills and competencies should be graded by ability. Many skill sets will work with each skill or competency, using three levels of ability:

Awareness—Has awareness of the knowledge/skill, and has completed the task at least once.

Practicing—Is able to follow a guide to complete a task.

Mastery—Is able to consistently perform the task without effort.

The following pages show a skill set created to track computer competencies.

Computers & Related Technologies

Awareness	Practicing	Mastery
Has awareness of the knowledge/skill, and/or has completed the task at least once.	Is able to follow a guide to complete the task.	Is able to consistently perform the task without effort.

Is able to load software.

print name	print name	print name
signature	signature	signature
date	date	date

Is able to manage files in a Windows environment.

print name	print name	print name
signature	signature	signature
date	date	date

Is able to create and send e-mail.

print name	print name	print name
signature	signature	signature
date	date	date

Is able to use a word processing package.

print name	print name	print name
signature	signature	signature
date	date	date

Is able to use electronic spreadsheets.

print name	print name	print name
signature	signature	signature
date	date	date

Is able to use presentation software.

print name	print name	print name
signature	signature	signature
date	date	date

Is able to access the Internet and the World Wide Web using a browser and/or specific address.

print name	print name	print name
signature	signature	signature
date	date	date

Is able to send files via modem.

print name	print name	print name
signature	signature	signature
date	date	date

 Template

A blank skill set is included on the accompanying diskette. Use it as a starting point for creating your own skill sets. **(Skillset.doc)**

The style of the skill set shown above allows you to track your progress on achieving your goals and increasing your skill levels. This skill set features space for a professional or educator to sign off on your level of ability. It is important that you take responsibility for getting your skills measured and signed off on. This is especially critical if you do not have a lot of work samples to support those skills. It is always more difficult to get a signature after the employment or class is over, since the person being asked to sign off may not have as clear a memory of the work. Be sure to request biographical information at the time of signature so you can include the information on a Faculty and Employer Biography sheet.

Creating Your Own Skill Sets

Getting started is easy. . . but takes some time.

- **Use job descriptions to identify skills you want to have—**
  Not all job descriptions are well written; however, there are
  usually key abilities identified in the text. Shop through the
  job requirements and evaluate your skills against those,
  looking for terminology. In fact, a really great way to evaluate your own skills is to write the job description for your
  ideal position and then check if you meet the qualifications.
  The Career Development office at your local community college, university, or professional association may be of some
  assistance if you are not quite sure where to look for job
  descriptions.

- **Use the "Want Ads" or job postings to identify and check
  skills—**Want ads in the newspaper or on the Internet tend to
  be brief because they are paid for by the word. However, this
  does not devalue the interesting information about the jobs
  that are available. Look at the skills, written and implied.
  Often it is right in front of you. Check the Sunday papers for
  job advertisements.

Now expand and refine this list of skills...

- **List the things you have done on the job—**If the majority
  of your work experience is as an hourly employee (line-level)
  then you need to reflect on a "day in your life." If the
  majority of your work experience is as a supervisor, then you
  need to reflect on a "week in your life." If the majority of your
  work experience is as a manager, then you need to reflect on
  a "month in your life." List all the things you do in the
  course of a day . . . week . . . month. This usually covers
  your routine skills. Break your time down so you can clearly
  think through the entire period of time. Your list should be
  of tasks and activities that you do. Try to be very specific;
  rather than saying, "as a supervisor I work with people to
  prepare food for the restaurant," consider also your
  responsibility for sanitation, coaching employees, and
  ensuring the standards of the operation. Can you do each
  person's job if asked? Many times we underestimate all the
  skills and tasks we do in a day.

- **List unique skills**—Things special to the position, those things you get asked to do because you are better at it than others. Focus on your creative skills, your problem-solving skills, and your ability to do several things at once.

- **List your transferable skills**—Those which can be used in many different positions. Consider your technology skills; more and more positions are specifically asking you to prove your computer skills and specific software expertise. Some companies are even giving skill tests to verify your abilities.

 **Ask the Expert**

No physical samples of my work!

Q. **What do I do if I don't have any good work samples? I don't generate a lot of physical materials in the job I'm doing now, I don't have any awards or community service to show, and I don't even have any good class projects or assignments to include. What do I do now?**

A. Start by exploring the skills you have. Make a list of all the skills you know you have. Then target people who can help you document your skills. Consider teachers, employers, and even personal references that hold good standing. Ask them to write you a letter of reference or participation. Take the time to guide them by letting them know exactly what skills you want them to address in their letters.

Another way to document your skills is by using a skill set. A skill set is a list of skills that have been grouped together. Make a list of your skill sets and ask your employers or instructors to sign off verifying your skills. It is best to use a combination of employers and instructors to help document your skills.

Get A Head Start...
Create Your Skill Sets in School or on the Job

Customize your skill sets based on your course work—While you are in school, take time at the beginning of each term to review the skills and competencies you expect to secure, refine, or learn about in each course. At the end of the project or class, you will have ability at the Awareness, Practicing, or Mastery levels. Imagine going into a class knowing what you want to get out of it and working with the instructor to create your own learning plan. You want to be in a position to be proactive rather than reactive to your education. This keeps you from being a "passive user" of the educational system. (Remember to keep good work samples for possible use later.)

Professionals on the job—At the beginning of a job or review period, you should clearly decide what skills you have, need, or want to prove, and which ones you want to develop during the next year. You need to give yourself enough structure so you can grow within the company and as a professional in your field. Consider incorporating your skill needs into your performance goals for the year. This is a good way to strategically organize yourself, especially if you make sure your goals and the company's goals interface or map back to each other.

Certifications, Diplomas, Degrees, or Awards

Remember, you need to prove the things you have done. Professional certificates related to areas of specialty, such as Novell certification, training certification, continuing education, workshops attended, distinctions, or accommodations are appropriate items to place in your portfolio. Here are some tips for using certificates and awards:

- **Include a copy of the certificate**—Include a quality photocopy or scanned image of the certificate or diploma as proof and verification. Don't include the original.

- **Include information about the organization presenting the certificate**—The certificate should be dated and have information about the organization. If it does not, add a page with the following items:
  - Name
  - Address and phone number of the organization
  - Any certification or licensing numbers given.

- **Place the most recent items first**—If you have any citations (not speeding or parking tickets!) for service, include them here in reverse chronological order with most current items coming first. For example, if you received the customer service award at work last year, and you received Dean's List this term—place the Dean's List before the customer service award.

- **Be selective**—What goes in here? Everything? No. Show items that will be of interest to your future employer. Do your homework on the interests of the organization with which you are applying or currently working for today. Remember that more is not necessarily better.

 Bright Idea!

Use color copies of originals and keep the original in a safe place. NEVER put the original copy of a project or certificate in your portfolio!

Community Service

There ARE Other Ways to Get Experience

You have not really worked in the area the potential employers are looking for . . . what can you do? Volunteer. People who are not actively in the work force or those people who have been out for a while can use their volunteer projects as a way to demonstrate skills and secure proof, without having held employment. Go to an organization and offer your services free of charge. Start a project and see it through to the end. Be sure to make it clear that all you want is a letter documenting your time and skills. Then have some fun and test drive, develop, or refine your skills.

Women or men who have stayed at home for a couple of years with their children often feel their skills are rusty. Prior to entering the work force, allow some time to do some structured volunteering. It could be as a fund-raiser or a kitchen supervisor at the YMCA. Seek out a not-for-profit organization and offer your professional skills. It doesn't matter if you are a mechanic, a cook, a graphic artist, or an accountant—offer the skills you feel you need help documenting. One woman was let go from a full-time marketing position because she didn't have the skills that were required in her changing job.While unemployed, she volunteered in the community, handling the marketing responsibilities for a local nonprofit organization. She used this experience to secure the skills her employer was looking for and was hired back. She used community service as a way of building her skills and proving her abilities.

In a recent meeting of industry recruiters, several said they look specifically for candidates with community service in their background. They believe individuals who volunteer will be willing to stay a little longer to get the project done; it signals an individual who is interested in giving back to, and not just taking from, the community—even the corporate community. Additionally, community service is another way to create positive public relations. Sometimes people are hired because of their volunteer connections and earned respect in the local or regional community. Other employers will require employees to do some community service such as Big Brother, Big Sister, little league coach, city council members, or serve as the Cancer Society or Heart Association chairperson.

Citizenship, ethics, and one's ability to balance his or her life is becoming more important. Volunteerism shows that you have a strategy for coping with on-the-job stress. Often recruiters are looking for ways of seeing balance in your life. Community service is one way to demonstrate this.

- It is appropriate to show work developed while serving with or on community organizations or associations. Examples might include photos of events you assisted with, copies of programs you helped develop or deliver, samples of the brochures, bylaws, or organizational pieces you developed. Remember, the organizations you associate with are a reflection on you—choose causes you are proud to be associated with over time.

- As your career progresses, you need to keep your samples up to date. Select your most significant contributions as well as those most current from the last 18 months.

Include pictures of your involvement in community service.

Don't underestimate this section of your portfolio. Here is your opportunity. The person reading your portfolio now has the chance to ask questions about you, your values and beliefs. Be sure you associate with causes you can support. It's important to understand the mission statement of the organization even if it's not printed on the brochure. Be prepared to answer questions about your service and about the association or organization.

Academic Plan of Study

You may be asking why you need to include an academic plan of study. The answer is really quite logical—you want to promote all the specialized education and/or training you have received. It also helps a current or potential employer distinguish between your background and that of other people in the same position. Your plan of study defines the courses you took to complete your degree. Remember that each school, college, or university has a distinct curriculum—you want your program to be known.

Look to course catalogs and transcripts for copies of your plan of study. Transcripts give course titles and grades; if your grades are not that great, don't volunteer the transcript. You should, however, indicate that it is available upon request. You can also use the description/presentation in the school bulletin or catalog. You need to show all your courses in your major and related area. Be sure to include the pages with the program, department, and degree description, as well as the title page and the date. You will find all of this especially helpful if you ever go back to school for an advanced degree.

Before you leave your school, get 10 copies of your transcript and find the copy of the course catalog that governed your degree. You may have to go back to your freshman boxes to find it. Keep the catalog or bulletin in a safe place, since these are often expensive to get if you need them in a hurry.

It may be appropriate to include the course descriptions from key classes. You may need to scan the information. Be sure to cite the date of the program and version of the catalog.

In an interview, the academic plan of study section is usually only referred to if needed and may even be overlooked when the person considering you is reviewing your portfolio. You need to have it in your portfolio, just in case.

Faculty and Employer Biographies

Faculty and employer bios are used to give you credibility. The person who signed your skill set sheets or letters of recommendation is giving his or her word that you have certain abilities. The faculty/employer bio sheet gives the interviewer background on who these people are and how they know you.

A faculty/employer bio sheet should include the following information:

- Name and job title
- Organization
- Contact information including address, phone/fax/e-mail
- Areas of specialty
- Date.

The arrangement of bios should be chronological. It is not necessary to repeat a bio for someone unless he or she has been promoted during the signature periods of your skill sets.

The bio sheet is placed under its own tabbed section in the portfolio, following Skill Areas and Works in Progress. This information can often be standardized and printed on labels.

 Template

A faculty and employer bio sheet can be found on the enclosed diskette. **(Faculty_Employer bios.doc)**

References

You will need three to five references that an employer can check. You should include character, academic, and employment references:

- **Character**—Someone you've worked with in the community, such as church, synagogue or mosque, not-for-profit organizations, clubs, and/or associations can provide good character references.
- **Academic**—Professors, teachers, counselors, coaches, and people who know your academic abilities can provide academic references.
- **Employment**—Supervisors, managers, human resource people at your current and previous positions can provide employment references.

It is never appropriate to use a peer, a subordinate, or a family member as a reference.

Sample Reference Sheet

David Morrow - References

Mr. Richard Brush
Lodging Department Chair
Hospitality College
Johnson & Wales University
Abbott Park Place
Providence, RI 02000
(123) 456-7890
Fax: (123)456-9870
E-mail: dbrush@provider.com
Home: (123) 456-4321 (hours: 6 p.m. to 9 p.m.)
(Academic Reference, Club Adviser)

Monsignor Robert McCaffrey
Providence Catholic Diocese
8800 Cathedral Square
Providence, RI 02000
Office: (123) 452-0987
Fax: (123) 452- 9876
(Personal Reference, Community Service)

Ms. Fran Bahmer
General Manager
Heartland Catering
RR1, Box 50
Bloomington, IL 61544
Office: (309) 663-0000
Fax: (309) 663-0001
(Employment Reference, Supervisor for three years; summer employment)

February, 2004

Include the person's name, full title, work address, work phone, fax, e-mail, and, if given permission, the person's home phone. Arrange all references on one page, and signal at the bottom of the reference the skills, competencies, or achievements the person can address. If you have more than three references, put them into two columns on the page.

You should be certain each of your references has a copy of your résumé and copies of work samples referred to them. As long as you keep them as a reference, you should forward them a copy of your résumé each time it is updated, with the changes highlighted.

 Template

A reference sheet is included on the diskette. (**References.doc**)

Proving Your Worth

Your work samples and support materials make up the largest portion of your portfolio. Take the time to save certificates, samples, and projects as you acquire them. Get into the habit of looking at your work and looking for samples. Take advantage of the moment and take photos of events and projects. Print just one more copy of that report and throw it into your portfolio file. If you don't have many work samples, request letters or recommendations or use skill sets to prove your worth. Once you have these elements together for your portfolio, you're almost ready to begin assembly. The next chapter will identify ways to use the portfolio to track certifications and will examine ways to show your commitment to your own professional growth.

CHAPTER 5

THE ASSEMBLY

Assembling the Portfolio

OK, you have all your stuff in piles and files—now what? Remember, the first chapter of this book gave you the big picture view on the portfolio. Chapters 2 to 4 gave you the gory details of each section in the portfolio (perhaps even more than you really wanted to know). This chapter will take you from the pieces to the whole finished product. You won't be ready to assemble until you first gather, sort, secure, and update your materials. We'll also take a look at special tips for assembling a Performance Portfolio for use in job reviews or promotion interviews.

Here are the five major steps to assembling your portfolio:

Step 1: Gather your supplies and documents.

Step 2: Sort and organize your work samples.

Step 3: Put them all together.

Step 4: Develop support materials.

Step 5: Check it out—proof it, test it.

Step 1 . . . Things to Gather

If you haven't already done so, read Chapters 1 to 4 of this book. Know what your goals and objectives are and how you plan to use your portfolio. Next, bring to one central location all your collected materials—consciously collect:

- Portfolio supplies—(see Chapter 1, "What Supplies Do I Need to Get Started?" or Chapter 9, Resource Guide)
- Your résumé
- Your work philosophy

- Your professional goals
- Your box of work samples... (Are there any old papers or projects that you can find or copy?)
- Certifications
- Degrees or diplomas
- Thank you letters or letters of recommendation
- Skill sets with signatures
- Faculty/employer bios
- Academic plans of study
- Professional membership cards and service samples
- Certification checklists
- Community service accommodations or service samples
- List of references
- And don't forget—your best friend.

Step #1 - Gather your materials ... and a friend

Assemble Your Portfolio BEFORE You Need It!

With all the work involved in creating a portfolio, it's easy to put it off until another day. If you decide not to choose this option of working in advance on the portfolio, please refer to the Emergency "I Need the Portfolio Now" instructions in Chapter 9, Resource Guide. We promise you'll need them. Even the authors of this book have had to choose between sleep and finishing a portfolio. Be prepared to clean off a big section of the floor for the assembly. If the floor cramps your style, use a table or large desk—just be prepared to find some space on a flat surface.

Step 2 . . . Sorting and Organizing Work Samples

Set Up Your Tabbed Areas

Use the job description, classified ad, and any other knowledge you have of the company or the position to prioritize the skills you will emphasize in your portfolio. Begin by selecting three to five main skill areas you want to emphasize and create a tab for each. Select categories which you can support with work samples. If you are a business major, for example, your tabs might be Management, Finance, and Communication. Now is the time to decide what other tabbed areas beyond work samples you want to use.

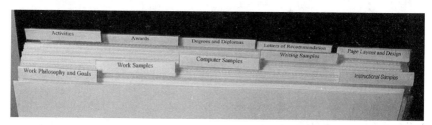

Step 2 - Select tabs that represent you.

Remember, this is your portfolio. You need to select the tabbed areas that best represent you. If you don't have any community service experiences, don't create a tab for it and then leave it blank. Don't struggle to find some activity or event to include just so you can write up two lines on a page. If you don't have it, don't include it! Play to your strengths. If you have only one sample for an area, consider grouping it with another sample from a different area and make a tab to reflect this. If you've been on the job for 10 years, you probably don't need to include a tab for Academic Plan of Study. If you can only come up with two really good tabbed areas, don't struggle to find a third and then include marginal samples. You are designing this portfolio to show off your strengths. Choose your tabbed areas to reflect this.

Select Samples

How do you decide which samples to use? Consider first the needs of the employer and look at the job ad to see what samples would be most effective. When sorting work and service samples, ask yourself:

- Which skills is the organization looking for in this position?
- What is your best work?
- Which samples show the most skills and competencies?
- Which work samples are the most interesting to you?
- Which work samples use more than text as an exhibit? Do any include pictures?
- Can you talk about your sample?

 Bright Idea!

Remember to select your best samples!

Consider using some of the following items as demonstrations of your skills and competency:

- Class projects
- Projects or reports demonstrating organization and professionalism
- Writing samples
- Computing samples
- Team efforts
- Certificates from workshops
- Performance appraisals (include internships/co-ops)
- Certifications
- Handouts
- Presentations
- Letters itemizing what you have accomplished.

Remember the Friend

Having a friend there to help you during assembly can be extremely important. Your friend is there to ask the "right" questions and to look at your portfolio from a "different angle." You may find that your friendship will be tested, especially if he or she does his/her job! Your friend's job is, of course, to ask you the really hard questions that push you to be your best. Your friend is also here to role play possible answers you may give the interviewer. Don't take things personally; give that friend honest answers even if they are not your best answers. You'll improve with practice.

Once you have organized your work samples you are then ready to develop the support materials that give your portfolio flow.

Step 3 . . . Putting It Together

Now that you have everything gathered, go ahead and put everything you've prepared into page protectors and into the 3-ring notebook. Organize your information into appropriate tabbed areas. Remember, we've included several documents on the accompanying diskette that can give you a starting point for creating your documents. Refer to Chapter 9, Resource Guide, for a complete listing of all templates.

- Begin with your **work philosophy** and **career goals**.
- Put your résumé in another page protector behind the work philosophy/goals page.
- Insert **skill sets** if used.
- Insert **letters of recommendation** where appropriate.
- Order your **work samples** and put them into page protectors. You may want to use connected page protectors to keep samples together. Order the work samples with your best examples first.
- Insert copies of **certifications**, **diplomas**, and **degrees**.
- Insert **community service samples**.
- Insert **professional membership** certificates and service samples.

- Insert **academic plan of study** and **faculty/employer bios**.
- Insert **references**.

Step 4 . . . Developing Support Materials

Now that you have the key elements inserted into the portfolio, it's time to create a few support materials.

Statement of Originality and Confidentiality

This one-page sheet should be placed at the beginning of your portfolio. It states that the portfolio is your work and indicates if certain portions of the portfolio should not be copied.

Statement of Originality and Confidentiality

This portfolio is the work of James Cook. Please do not copy without permission. Some of the exhibits, work samples, and/or service samples are the proprietary property of the organization whose name appears on the document. Each has granted permission for this product to be used as a demonstration of my work.

Sample Statement of Originality and Confidentiality

 Template

Use the document on the accompanying diskette to create your own page. **(stmt of originality.doc)**

Work Sample Overview Cards

A work sample overview card is a small card (the size of a business card) that contains a brief description of the work sample. Use sheets of blank business cards to print descriptive information about each sample you have within your portfolio. If you have electronic copies of a work sample, you may want to edit the file and insert a text box directly into the work sample to act as your overview card. This way, your overview card remains with the sample at all times.

You may encounter a situation where an electronic work sample does not fill an entire page. In these cases it is appropriate to add headers to the page (in addition to the overview card) briefly describing what the work sample represents. Whether you choose to print separate overview cards using business cards or insert electronic overview cards, each overview card should include certain details about the work sample:

- Title
- Purpose
- Date developed
- Names of team members who developed it
- Demonstrated skills in keyword format—use words that are emphasized on your résumé and heading.

Fund-Raising Brochure

Designed and produced brochure for
fund-raising marketing piece
- raised $125,000 - Spring 2004

Skills - Graphic Design, Color Printing,
Fund-Raising, Writing

Work Sample Overview Card

 Template

Use the template on the enclosed disk to create your own work sample overview cards. **(Work Sample Overview Cards.doc)**

Allow for Your Style

You are creating a document that represents you and your career to the world. Be sure it feels like you and is a tool you feel comfortable using. Some people make title pages for each section of their portfolios. You can use clip art, photos, and graphics to give the portfolio your own style. Just be sure the end result looks professional.

General Rules to Follow

- Put all papers into the page protectors using both the front and back
- Use colored paper to draw attention to special work or service samples
- Use the same type of paper on your résumé and references (prepare two extra sets of these documents to hand out during the interview)
- Proofread everything at least three times
- NEVER USE YOUR ORIGINALS.

Step 5 . . . Check It Out

We hope this was not an emergency assembly of your portfolio and that you have at least 12 hours to proof and let the portfolio cool. Here are a few items you should check and recheck:

- Read for typos, spelling, grammar, and format. If you are not good at this, have a friend do it.
- Talk through the sections of your portfolio with a friend, thinking about which parts you will elaborate on in an interview.
- When in doubt, take it out... if you are not sure or are not pleased with an item—leave it out.
- If you have assembled this portfolio for a particular interview, make sure you have selected work samples that meet the needs of the organization.

Assembling an On-the-Job Portfolio

When you have a job, your portfolio can help you keep it and get a pay increase or promotion. The overall organization of the portfolio is the same, except that work/service samples are organized in chronological order and your professional goals may be organized by your previous year's professional goals and objectives (or the time since your last appraisal).

- **Check your calendar**—Get in the habit of writing down the start dates, benchmarks, and completion dates of projects. Write down in your calendar any letters of acknowledgment or awards received. Months from now you will have a road map ready to read and secure your documentation for the portfolio.

- **Once a month make two lists of what you have accomplished, planned and unplanned**—If you can't do it once a month, then take 30 minutes once every 90 days and think about your career. Make the appointment with yourself right now; map out the appointments and keep them.

- **Set up a file box or file drawer**—At the end of each project, make a second copy of it and put it in your file. At the very least, save it on a disk. Remember that setting aside a copy of your work needs to become reflex; it will save you a lot of chasing when you put together your actual portfolio.

- **Review the job description for your position**—As far in advance of the review as possible, reread the job description of your position. It is good to strategically consider your level of skill in each of the position statements. Use the job description to guide your quest for work samples and skill set documentation. You may even want to consider seeking out certifications that will document and help you recover from any deficits.

   If you don't have a specific job description for your position (and many people don't), the solution is simple. Write one now. Give a copy of your job description to your supervisor and seek his or her input. It is helpful and strategic to establish the criteria of your position before your review.

- **Review the performance appraisal standards before the actual review**—It seems simple, but be sure you understand the "rules of the game" at the beginning of the performance period. This may or may not be possible. Some organizations have very general standards or criteria. It is especially necessary in these cases that you develop your career portfolio and utilize it for the review. Now that you know the specifics, keep them in the back of your mind as you make decisions on your work samples and career activities.

- **Concentrate on your skill sets, your work samples, and professional activities**—The other parts of the portfolio, such as your work philosophy, goals, résumé, awards, and certificates, should appear in your portfolio but not be emphasized. The other sections serve as background and quite often serve as subtle support to refresh the reviewer's knowledge of you.

- **Write documentation for other people the way you would like to receive it**—Remember the key elements of good documentation: timeframe, skills demonstrated, people on the team, attitude of the individual, and suggestions for future projects based on this work.

- **Put it all together**—Put together this year's work in chronological order or into the major areas set up in your job description. Then be sure to explain to the person reviewing you that you have put together a self-review. Set your supervisor up to utilize your career portfolio. Never simply walk in the door with your portfolio; it could be perceived as a threat.

Congratulations—You Have a Career Portfolio!

Whew!! Assembly is a lot of work. If you've gotten to this point and have a finished portfolio in hand, congratulate yourself. You've taken a huge step toward understanding yourself and you're ready to take your portfolio to the marketplace. You have taken time to examine your beliefs and goals and had the opportunity to evaluate your work, your skills, your strengths and weaknesses. You've searched through and found the best examples of your work and you now have a tool for tracking your career.

In the next chapter, we'll look at how you can adapt your portfolio into an electronic portfolio. If you want to explore the new frontier of Internet websites and find ways to create new opportunities, read on. If you can't wait to learn how to actually use your portfolio in an interview or review, go on to Chapter 7, The Portfolio in Action ... Getting the Job.

Congratulations on Your Portfolio!

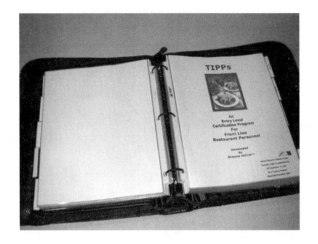

The finished portfolio involves a lot of hard work!

CHAPTER 6

THE ELECTRONIC PORTFOLIO

Technology "Levels the Playing Field"

What exactly is an electronic career portfolio? It is a personalized, career-oriented website that you use to get a job or to make your skills known. It can be accessed from the Internet, or you can control access to the portfolio by putting it on a disk or CD-ROM. The electronic career portfolio contains the same information as your "hard copy" portfolio, but it is organized and accessed differently. Consider this... one is linear, like a newspaper which is read one page after the other—the hard-copy one; and one is nonlinear, or organized in such a way that you can mix up the order and still make sense, like a website—the electronic career portfolio.

Electronic portfolios can be stored on a CD-ROM, zip, or floppy disk.

Why Would I Want an Electronic Portfolio?

"It takes long enough to develop a hard copy portfolio, why would I want to spend all my time developing a website to do the same thing?" You're asking the right question. The beauty of the Electronic Portfolio is its ability to:

- **Cluster ideas that are related**—Consider using the same work sample but showing your link in two or more skill sets. For example, you may have a report you generated which demonstrates your leadership ability, knowledge of technology, and training skills. If you have separate pages for leadership, technology, and training, you can reference the same sample from each page. You are able to dial in the user to the exact parts of the work sample with the electronic portfolio.

- **Search by keywords using buttons or frames**—Employers like to scan quickly and get a lot of information.

- **Add more of yourself**—as your voice or a video clip. Short sound bites allow you to "show yourself in action." Keep in mind that these files can be big and work fine on a CD but may be too big or take too long for access on a web connection.

- **Follow up your interview with support material**—It is appropriate to leave a "copy" of your career portfolio in electronic form for an interviewer to review at a later time.

- **Provide new and different work samples that supplement your hard copy portfolio**—You can include more work samples in the electronic portfolio that support your paper portfolio.

So... Do I Even Need a Paper Career Portfolio?

Oh, yes! The hard copy and the electronic portfolio include the same elements, but people process, view, and explore the information differently. The paper (hard copy) portfolio and the electronic portfolio work differently in the career market.

Hard Copy Portfolios

- Hard copies work better in interviews. They are more flexible and easier to manage in an interview setting. They allow you to interact with the interviewer in a personal way.

- Some people may not have access or be comfortable using a computer.

- It is usually faster to make changes to a hard copy portfolio by switching out work samples to meet the needs of an interview. It takes more time to adjust the contents of an electronic portfolio.

When Does the Electronic Portfolio Become Attractive?

- As follow up after a successful interview—so others who did not get time to spend with you can be SOLD on you

- When they want more time with you after the interview to learn even more about you

- It is something they can view without time restrictions

- It is a perk that you have some technology literacy

- It is a support vehicle—it is not the primary source.

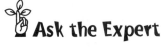 Ask the Expert

When to use an electronic portfolio

Q. **Is it appropriate to use an electronic portfolio during an interview?**

A. Typically you do not use an electronic portfolio during an interview unless you are interviewing for a position in the tech field. The paper portfolio lends itself best to the needs of an interview. There are three ways a paper portfolio is used in an interview:

1. Offer your portfolio at the beginning of an interview for the interviewer to review

2. Use your portfolio to answer a question during your interview

3. Use your portfolio as a summary or review at the end of the interview.

An electronic portfolio is best used during the pre-interview process by noting on your cover letter that you have a portfolio available for preview . It can also be an effective tool after an interview as a summery.

Some things to keep in mind regarding your electronic portfolio include:

• Make it easy to navigate, set it up to automatically execute

• Be sure to attach the directions for launching the electronic portfolio

• Common platforms for an electronic portfolio include using Power Point slides or HTML (web page) formats.

Electronic Portfolios Work Differently

Electronic portfolios are used differently than printed ones—you can't expect the person to whom you are showing it to run and get his/her laptop. You can, however, use it as the copy you leave with the interviewer to support your printed copy. People process information differently, and tabbed work samples and statements support what you say. With the electronic portfolio and the nonlinear approach, you can never be sure in what order people will view your info—so it becomes more important that it be able to stand alone and is organized into chunks.

Wait! I'm not a "Techno-Wizard"— How Can I Do This?

If you're feeling a little intimidated right now, thinking you don't have the skills or ability to design a website or something really technical... relax. There are several ways to get this accomplished and it doesn't have to cost a lot. You are either going to design this website yourself or you're going to get someone to help you. There are actually many easy-to-use programs for designing websites where you don't have to know any "code" or "HTML" stuff, and some are even free.

Stay focused on your goal. If you have problems "coding" or getting something to work like a graphic or a table or a form, call in your "tech" buddies or friends for help. Don't let the technology manage you. Don't give up. Local universities have plenty of places with lab assistance. Check out job boards and find a person who is looking for a way to get more web development experience for their portfolio!

No Coding!!!

Students! Check your computer lab resources to see what programs are already available! Microsoft FrontPage is an easy-to-use program for creating web pages. You can also create web pages in Microsoft Publisher and Microsoft Word.

Getting It All Together

- **What do you already have on disk?**—Find projects, reports, presentations, budgets, etc., that you already have in electronic format.

- **Get the rest of your documents into electronic format—** (Take your tote box to a friend with a scanner!) This can take some time, so allow half a day or so for this task.

- **Get yourself an electronic suitcase**—Find a way to store all these files. You can put files on several diskettes, a Zip disk, a writable/rewritable CD-ROM disk, or have someone burn a CD-ROM disk for you with all your samples.

- **Get the software you will use to develop the web page and figure out how to use it**—(or get your techno friend to help).

- **Not all work samples belong on your electronic portfolio**—Prioritize and choose your best samples. You may need to customize your electronic portfolio for a potential employer, so scan all of your work samples.

- **Now you're ready to design your site!**

Designing the Electronic Career Portfolio

- Start with a solid, working hard copy career portfolio.
- Consider your style and your "look," including:
  - ◆ Fonts
  - ◆ White space
  - ◆ Graphics and photos.
- Decide how you will structure the items to be used including Work Samples, Work Philosophy, Goals, Résumé, References, Certificates, etc. Will they go on separate pages, or will some of them be together?
- Use templates and wizards where possible.
- Choose the work samples—remember that you can organize them in a nonlinear way.
- Storyboard the electronic portfolio; that is to say, take a large sheet of paper and colored markers or pencils and draw pictures of what you want where and what links or references you want on the contained pages. If you have access to a classroom or boardroom, use the chalk or white board. Take a good look here at how much information you want to give in the "big" picture. How much information do you want to have connected and how do you want the people to navigate or move through your portfolio? Consider using basic web HTML editors.
- Design the site on your computer.
- Test it to make sure it works. Pull in a few friends and have them take a look. Revise the site as needed.
- Write the instructions for executing the files. Attach them to the holder of your disk or the cover letter with your website.
- Then go for it—electronically produce the portfolio, date, and make copies. If you have to acquire a new skill, consider how it will support you in your career. In today's world most people are used to navigating a website and understand how they work.
  - Once you've developed a website on your computer you need to get it from your computer to the Internet. Keep in mind that when it's on the Internet, everyone can access it unless you know how to password protect it.

- You need to find a host for your website. There are a lot of free or inexpensive ways. First, check with your Internet service provider (ISP) to see if you can put up a free personal website—many ISPs include a "personal" site as part of your monthly fee. You can also get space on other sites. Many colleges and universities offer free web space for every student.

How do I put it on the Internet?

- Get an ISP—find a spot on the web to "host" your website
- Create your web pages on your computer
- Upload or FTP the files to the Internet site.

Upload Your Files

- Once you've got a place to put your site, you need to "upload" your files from the computer to the web. This process is called FTPing, or publishing your files.
- You will be given a user name and password that will allow you to upload the files to a specific location on the website. To update the site you make changes to the pages on your computer and then upload the files to the web. If you know how to copy and paste files between directories on a computer, you can update your site. If you need assistance, find a friend to help.

Maintaining Your Site

- Put up current work samples as you create them.
- Don't forget to take it down. When you get the job or achieve the goal it may be time to take down your site. You don't want to generate "business" if you're unable to accept it.

 **Ask the Expert**

Publicizing your site

Q. **Should I include the web address in my résumé?**

A. It depends on how well dialed in you are to this particular employer. It's very tempting on the electronic portfolio to put more there than you need. You still need to strategically design the website to meet the needs of the employer.

Making the Most of Your Electronic Portfolio

In all cases, electronic or paper, the career portfolio is a tool for demonstrating who you are and what knowledge and skills you have—use the portfolio to help people learn about you and your attitude. The mental process of developing a career portfolio is the same for a paper hard copy and an electronic portfolio. The real benefit of the electronic portfolio is the ability to give people more time to access your portfolio. For examples of electronic portfolios visit our website **http://learnovation.com.**

The following pages show pages from a student electronic portfolio. This site was created in Macromedia's Dreamweaver, but you can easily create web pages in Microsoft Publisher, Microsoft Word, and Microsoft FrontPage. You can see this student website online at **http://learnovation.com/egportfolio/default.htm**.

Note: Portions of this electronic portfolio sample have been modified or edited for learning purposes.

 Template

The enclosed disk contains a directory called **e_portfolio**. It contains nine HTML pages you can use to create and customize your own career portfolio. The following pages are included: home/opening page, work philosophy and goals, résumé, four blank skill area pages that can be customized to your specific skill areas, awards, and community service. The style of the pages is similar to the examples on the next few pages. Feel free to change the layout, colors, and information included to create your own unique portfolio.

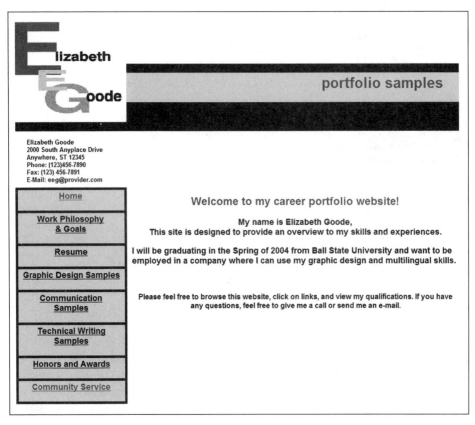

Home page

The Home page of your website serves as a starting point for the electronic portfolio. It introduces who you are and serves to orient the viewer to your website. Navigation buttons help the

viewer easily go between the pages in the website. Underlined text are links to additional pages. The user can click on the text to go to a related page. It is a good idea to put your contact information on the home page, or on a separate contact page.

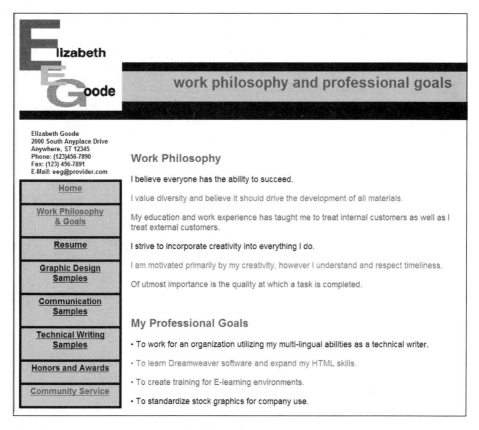

Work Philosophy and Goals page

This page lists Elizabeth's work philosophy and goals. This should be one of the first things a person sees when viewing your electronic portfolio. You may choose to list the work philosophy and goals on your home page. You might also decide to add some simple clip art to make a page more interesting. Be sure any clip art you use is related to the items on the page.

resume

Elizabeth Goode
2000 South Anyplace Drive
Anywhere, ST 12345
Phone: (123)456-7890
Fax: (123) 456-7891
E-Mail: eeg@provider.com

Print a copy
(PDF)

Home

Work Philosophy
& Goals

Resume

Graphic Design
Samples

Communication
Samples

Technical Writing
Samples

Honors and Awards

Community Service

Elizabeth Goode

2000 South Anyplace Drive • Anywhere, ST 12345
Phone: (123) 456-7890• Fax: (123) 456-7891 • E-Mail: eeg@provider.com

Skills and Qualities

- Self-motivated, creative, problem solver with a "can-do" attitude
- Flexible in ability to participate in, or lead on long- and short-term projects
- Skilled in both PC and Macintosh environments
- Able to quickly learn and adapt to new software
- Skilled in the following applications and languages:

Windows '98 & 2000 & XP • Adobe Illustrator • QuarkXPress • Adobe InDesign
Adobe PhotoShop • Adobe Acrobat Exchange • Xerox Elixir Software Suite • MS Word
MS Excel • MS PowerPoint • MS Access • Word Perfect • FrontPage • HTML
Lotus 1-2-3 • Internet Explorer • Netscape Navigator • Hotmail • Groupwise • MS Outlook

Education

Bachelor of Arts - Ball State University, Muncie, IN
Major: English and Japanese • Minor: Business Operating Systems
Anticipated Graduation – May 2004

Associates of Arts: May 2002 - IUPUI Herron School of Art, Indianapolis, IN
Visual Communications – major

Employment

Electronic Publisher (part-time)
USA Group/Sallie Mae - 2001 – Present

- **Created original art pieces** for use in intranet pages and internal communications
- **Designed** posters, flyers, invitations, postcards, brochures, slide shows, envelopes, letterheads, manuals, and business cards for internal clients
- **Designed paper, electronic, and mainframe-compatible forms** in a full print production environment; preparing artwork and print specifications to vendors to meet clients needs
- **Performed client outreach presentations** detailing departmental capabilities
- **Initiated an electronic, paperless process** to reduce waste and cost.

Quality Control Coordinator
USA Group 2001

- **Tracked and coordinated all department jobs** from request through approval and delivery
- **Coordinated with purchasing and external vendors** to fill customer orders in a timely and cost effective manner
- **Proofread and edited all forms** for style and compliance to Corporate Communication Guidelines.

Tutor of Reading and Study Skills
Ball State University 2000 - 2001

- **Performed desktop publishing duties:** creating flyers, posters, worksheets, and data reports
- Tutored ESL clients in reading English, composition, conversational skills, and related tasks.
- Edited and reviewed book drafts and documents geared to ESL learners.

Retail Salesperson
Educational Materials Kelso's/Education Galore 1998 - 1999

- Created original and unique displays for seasonal stock
- Self supervising, key-holding sales person responsible for opening, closing, preparing back deposits, scheduling, intra-company communication and fielding customer complaints.

Résumé page   *(continued)*

Résumé - (continued)

The résumé page looks very similar to Elizabeth's hard copy résumé. She has added colored headings and included links to work samples in other areas of the electronic portfolio. If you click on the invitations link under the job title Electronic Publisher, you will go to the graphic design samples page.

The formatting of the online résumé takes up more space and if you print the web page, you may lose some of the information from the printed page. Elizabeth has included a graphic of a printer that is linked to a PDF copy of her one-page résumé. When you click the printer, a new browser window will open and display a printable version of her portfolio in Acrobat Reader. The person viewing the electronic portfolio must have Acrobat Reader installed on their machine in order to view the printable résumé. Acrobat Reader is available for free from Adobe. Most new computers come with Acrobat Reader already installed. In order to make a PDF file, you need to have a copy of the complete Adobe Acrobat on your computer.

The next several pages of the electronic portfolio are Elizabeth's key skill areas. These are the skills she is trying to promote to potential employers. She has grouped work samples by area. She has included smaller graphics (sometimes called thumbnails) of her work samples on each page. If the viewer wants to see a larger copy, they can click on the sample, or on the underlined link, and a new window will open with a larger version of the sample.

As with a hard copy portfolio, you should put your most important and best work samples first. You should also organize your key areas, so your strongest area is the first in the site navigation.

Elizabeth
Goode

graphic design samples

Elizabeth Goode
2000 South Anyplace Drive
Anywhere, ST 12345
Phone: (123)456-7890
Fax: (123) 456-7891
E-Mail: eeg@provider.com

Graphic design excites me the most.

It allows me to be as creative as I choose while delivering an important message

I believe knowledge can be transferred and enhanced
through art and interesting layout and design.

This is where I truly shine!

| Home |
| Work Philosophy & Goals |
| Resume |
| Graphic Design Samples |
| Communication Samples |
| Technical Writing Samples |
| Honors and Awards |
| Community Service |

College Fair Promotion

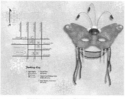

USA Group Invitation

(click items to enlarge)

Invitation and Poster- USA Group

Promotional
Poster

Promotional
Flyer

Key Skill Area - Graphic Design

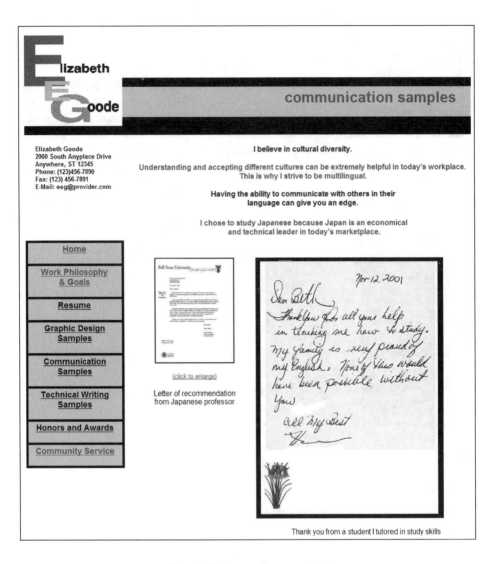

Key Skill Area - Communication

Additional work samples could include reports, project summaries, slides, and presentations. Remember that the web is a more graphic environment. People get bored very easily with loads of heavy text. Use graphics and clip art to make your site more appealing.

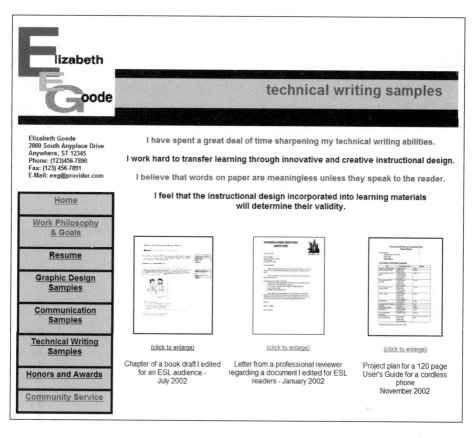

Key Skill Area - Technical Writing

When you click on any of these work samples, a new browser window will open and a PDF version of the file will display. Using smaller versions of a graphic saves space and browsing time for the viewer.

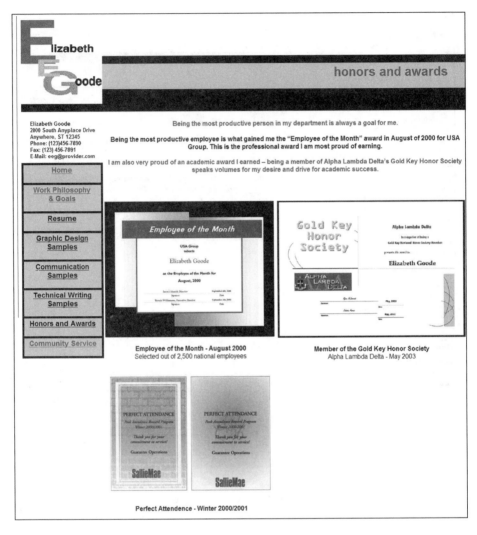

Honors and Awards

Don't forget to include graphics or photos of honors and awards you've received. Remember, the goal is to show the viewer what sets you apart from others.

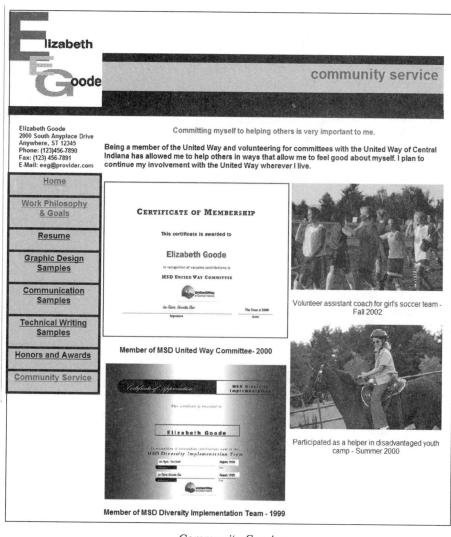

Community Service

Community service is a great place to include certificates and photos of people in action. Don't forget to include graphics and pictures when you can. It makes the electronic portfolio more interesting and draws the viewer into the portfolio.

If you've taken the time to create an electronic portfolio, give youself a pat on the back—you deserve it! Electronic portfolios give you more flexibility and more opportunities to show your skills and talents, but it takes time and effort to produce an electronic portfolio.

Don't forget that electronic portfolios are often used to give an employer another look at your skills, or to emphasize something you forgot you had. It may be just that extra effort and initiative that gets you into the job you want.

CHAPTER 7

THE PORTFOLIO IN ACTION: GETTING THE JOB

Now That I Have It, How Do I Use It?

Now that you have the portfolio, what do you do with it? It looks good, feels nice, and you survived the assembly process. You may be wondering "How do I use this portfolio?" and "How do I let them (the interviewer or boss) know that I have it?" This chapter talks about using your portfolio:

- To set the interviewer up to look at your portfolio
- As an overview of your abilities
- To answer a question
- To get a co-op or externship position
- To demonstrate your abilities in a performance review
- To obtain a promotion.

Interview Techniques

Your portfolio is finished... you have assembled work samples and support materials to help you prove to a potential employer that you are the right person for the job. Now, how do you use it? The first thing you need to do is test drive your portfolio before your first interview.

Good marketing is required of you and your work. Promote your portfolio ahead of time by placing a note at the bottom of your résumé: *Professional Portfolio Available upon Request.* You should also refer to the portfolio in your cover letter and on phone interviews when communicating with a company. Your portfolio is one of the prominent tools you take to the interview.

Get Comfortable with Your Portfolio

After assembling the portfolio, you should be intimately acquainted with it. You should know the contents of each tabbed area and be able to explain the significance of each piece of the portfolio. You should be able to tell the interviewer your work philosophy and goals without looking, and you should be able to turn to any work sample and talk about it: what it represents, how it was created, what skills you used during the process, the people involved in developing it, and what you learned from the project. The order of the tabbed areas should be second nature so you aren't flipping through the pages trying to find a particular sample or a certain skill set.

Grab a friend and test drive your portfolio before you need it!

When you can comfortably navigate your portfolio, it's time to try it out on someone else. Grab a friend (preferably the one who helped you assemble your portfolio) and go through a few "mock" interviews. Have your friend ask you common interview questions and practice using the portfolio to provide the answers. You should also practice explaining at the beginning of an interview that you have a portfolio of your work and exactly what that is.

Customize as Needed

Next, you need to get ready for your first interview. You need to research the company and the position and have a good idea of the requirements of the job. You should be able to identify what strengths you bring to the position and what challenges you may have to face, in terms of experience or education needs. This is the time to customize your portfolio to the needs of the potential employer.

- If you customized the career objective on your résumé for this company, be sure the copy in your portfolio matches the copy sent to the company.

- You may want to tweak your career goals slightly to take into account any special needs or opportunities presented by the employer.

- Customize your work samples based on the position and the company. If this position requires good training skills, you may want to pull in that training program sample you developed for a management class or a training outline you used when you taught customer service skills. If it is focusing on management skills, you might insert a copy of SWOT analysis or the project timelines you developed on your internship. Choose the work samples that will help you connect with the interviewer. Be prepared to show them why you are the person for the position.

Working the Portfolio in the Interview

During the interview, it's important to let the interviewer know within the first 15 minutes that you have a portfolio available. Watch the interviewer for signals of interest. Use the portfolio to set up the interviewer to ask you the questions you want to answer and that you can answer best. If you are offered the opportunity to overview your portfolio, be conscious of time. In a 30-minute interview you should be able to overview your portfolio in five to eight minutes, unless there are questions being asked.

Orient the interviewer to your portfolio.

Actually showing the portfolio may seem physically awkward. You may be sitting opposite the person by the time you are ready to show the portfolio. You may want to get up and stand beside the person to talk briefly through the sections. Make sure your head is not above the interviewer's head. Kneel or bend down to accomplish this. Usually the person viewing it will already be seated. It's difficult to read upside down, so get up and stand next to the person or people interviewing you. (A gentle reminder—women should pay attention to their necklines when leaning over. Both men and women should be sure their deodorant is working!) If getting up and moving around is not feasible or comfortable for you, you can work the portfolio across a desk. Just be sure the interviewer can clearly see the contents of the portfolio.

- **Begin by overviewing your work philosophy and professional goals**—This shows you have plans and focus—spend a little time here.

- **Point out your résumé and remind the person that he or she already has a copy**—Of course you should have a spare résumé tucked in the inside pocket of the portfolio.

- **For each additional section, describe briefly what the viewer or reader will find**—Let the viewer determine how much detail to go into in each section.

- **Don't use the portfolio to shut off questions from the recruiter**—Give enough overview to pique the person's curiosity so he or she can ask better questions of you. When you're finished showing the portfolio, leave it in front of the person.

Ask the Expert

Interviewing advice

Q. **I am about to graduate from college and am setting up interviews with potential employers. What is your BEST advice for interviewing to help me set myself apart from other applicants?**

A. Your career portfolio is a great tool to strengthen an interview. It does a couple of things: first, it helps to guide those interviewers who may not be especially good at conducting interviews, by showing them your work samples and giving insight into you. Second, it helps people, who are not perhaps as outgoing, to anticipate questions as well as to use props to answer. The process of assembling a portfolio gets you to review what you have to offer and to organize it into categories that can increase what you are worth to an employer. When you are asked questions in the interview, you can then show and tell what you know—allowing your work to do some of the speaking for you. Assembling your work samples into key skill areas is the first place to start. Dialing into the culture and goals of the organization also helps one to choose work samples for effectiveness. Community service is also a way to show how well you work with people and contribute to the community.

Emphasis on Course Work

If within the first five minutes of the interview the person has not expressed an interest in the portfolio, be prepared to use it as a means for answering a specific question. It should be easy to answer these questions because you had to answer the same types of questions when you developed your portfolio. Use your classroom projects and course materials to demonstrate your abilities. Here are some questions that lead themselves to be answered by a look at your portfolio:

- **"What are your five-year goals?"** or **"What are your future plans?"** (See the work philosophy and professional goals section.)
- **"How confident are you on the computer?"** (See the work/service samples with projects that are computer-generated, demonstrating the software and skills they want to see such as spreadsheets, word processing and database project, or any specialty software.)
- **"What do you do for recreation or release?"** (Show them your community service section.)
- **"What was your most difficult class?"** (Show them a work sample from your class.)
- **"Have you ever . . . ?"** (Fill in the blank and show the person a work or service sample.)
- **What certifications do you hold?** (See the certifications, diplomas, and degrees sections.)
- **"How do you work as part of a team?"** (Show them work samples that you generated as a group project and discuss the group dynamics.)

Don't be surprised if the interviewer asks to see the entire portfolio and not just the one section you are showing him or her.

Reactions...

You may find the interviewer has never heard about using a portfolio before. Additionally, he or she may not have the time to view it or he or she may be on a tight time schedule and have a list of fixed questions to address. Try to use your portfolio to answer questions. This can often spark the interest of the interviewer. On the other hand, you may find yourself leading the interview through the use of your portfolio. If you are being interviewed by several people in a group setting, you may find the interviewers fight over the opportunity to see your portfolio first. You may be in a situation where you are talking to one person and another person is looking at your portfolio. Using the work sample overview cards in each page can help a person understand the contents of your portfolio without your aid. This may be helpful.

Normally, you will be able to find some way to work the portfolio into the interview or review. However, if you do not spark the interviewer's interest, even after a clear offering and explanation of what the portfolio is, trust your instincts. It may be that going through the process improved your interviewing skills enough that they are intimidated by your organization.

Leaving Your Portfolio

If you have sparked the curiosity of the interviewer with your portfolio, he or she may ask you leave it with the company overnight so they can review it in more detail. If this is feasible and you have no other interviews in the time frame, it may be a great opportunity to reinforce your abilities to the interviewer. Make sure you clearly arrange a time to pick up the portfolio when he or she has finished reviewing it. If you have an electronic copy of your portfolio, you may want to leave a copy with the interviewer at the end of the interview.

Be sure you have placed copies of all your original documents in your portfolio. Don't include sensitive or proprietary information in your portfolio, as some organizations feel free to copy your portfolio. In order to manage this, be sure you include the Statement of Originality and Confidentiality at the beginning of your portfolio.

After It's Over...

Take time after your interview to debrief. Were they interested in your portfolio? Did you feel rushed in presenting it? Did it stay shut in your lap during the whole interview? Think about how you used it and how you can improve. Keep these things in mind for your next interview.

Be sure to follow up with a thank-you letter to the interviewer. Thank-you letters should be relatively brief, thanking the interviewer for his or her time. Try to include some personal comment that will help the interviewer remember you. Comments about your portfolio may help jog their memory.

Getting the Internship or Co-Op Experience

Internships and co-op experiences are an important part of your education in many fields of study. You gain practical experience while working in your desired field and make connections with a potential full-time employer. In general, nine out of ten internships lead to full-time job offers with the company. As in a regular job interview, the company is trying to decide why they should hire you and how you can help them. Your portfolio can be a valuable asset in proving your worth. It can set you apart from the other applicants and show your preparation and commitment to the industry. Your portfolio can be important in fields such as accounting, where there may be fierce competition for a limited number of internship positions.

Writing Goals and Learning Agreements

You can use your portfolio to set up learning agreements and set goals for your internship or co-op. A **learning agreement** is a list of goals and objectives you plan to achieve while employed as an intern. You indicate the skills you want to acquire, the employer determines the work that needs to be accomplished, and the faculty member sets up a system for recording a grade. You may want to create a specialized skill set sheet to record the skills you want to take away from the experience. You can use the skill sheet to track your progress and document your abilities. You can have the employer sign off on your level of ability, and then use the skill set as a vehicle for evaluating your performance on the job.

Setting Up a Track Record

An internship or co-op experience is an excellent way to collect work samples and certifications for your portfolio. Use your portfolio to track project timelines and chart your progress toward your goals. Contract with the employer telling them about your portfolio and your need for concrete work samples. You will probably find them very happy to accommodate your needs. Having an employee who is dialed into accomplishing specific goals and objectives will certainly be a positive experience for them as well!

Once You Have the Job

If you are offered a permanent position with the employer, congratulations! You are now ready to shift your portfolio from a job-hunting tool to a professional review and promotion tool. You can use the portfolio to track your achievement on the job and progress on your professional goals.

Use the portfolio to track your quarterly and annual goals at work. Keep track of the projects you are involved in, committees you've served on, professional development seminars you have attended, and any other professional opportunities. You'll still want to track your community service involvement and any personal certifications and education you pursue on your own time.

Using the Portfolio for Reviews and Promotions

When it's time for your quarterly review, you'll want to overview your accomplishments over the last period and get your portfolio ready to go. If you've kept copies of your projects and activities during the quarter, you should be ready for your review. Tell your boss about your portfolio and offer to let him or her review it several days prior to the review. This can help the interviewer prepare better questions and have time to reflect on all your accomplishments. Sometimes it's amazing to see how much you have really accomplished! As you grow professionally, your goals and work philosophy will also change. Make sure you keep this updated and current.

Now that you know how to use the portfolio during your performance review, let's talk about how to use it during the reviews where you are up for a promotion. A promotion may be a new title, new assignment to a different branch of the organization, or simply progression within the company hierarchy. In any of these cases, your portfolio should reflect your work from the period of your last promotion. If that was two years ago, then your work should reflect the last two years. If you have not been promoted yet, have your portfolio reflect your work from the time you began your employment.

Work samples, should be just that—samples—not everything you ever did. Just as in the career portfolio, you need to choose highlights of your best work. Even if something is not able to fit on an 8.5" x 11" sheet of paper, you should still include it. You might want to include a summary sheet in your portfolio and indicate the full project is available for review. Your choices should summarize as many skills as possible and as much professional growth as possible. In these cases it may be appropriate to include prior good reviews as evidence of your wonderful performance, which is, of course, deserving of the reward of a pay increase and/or the "corner office."

The Portfolio in Action

As you work with your portfolio in more interview settings, you'll come to appreciate how much your portfolio can add to the mix. You really can show off your skills and abilities to the best of your advantage. Once you have the job, you can transition your portfolio to track your professional life at work. Remember, your portfolio is a tool for life—your life and your career. Success!

CHAPTER 8

A MATTER OF STYLE

You are a professional, you have the credentials and the confidence to get ahead. You need to make sure your portfolio projects the same impression. If your portfolio looks sloppy and disorganized, don't even bother to take it to the interview or meeting. Your portfolio must look as clean, organized, and professional as you do.

The focus of this section is on style: the look, feel, and presentation of the materials in the portfolio. This section provides some basic guidelines for producing your work samples and other documents in your portfolio by taking a look at:

- Working with words and pictures (text and graphics)
- Production tips for video and photography
- Physical production of materials using copiers, scanners, and printers.

Text

Have you ever been reading something and suddenly you realize that you have no idea what you just read for the last four pages? This happens to all of us, but why? Are we not concentrating hard enough, or is the material boring? Your goal in creating your career portfolio is to keep the person reading it awake and interested. You need to make sure the information is easy to understand, well organized, and presented in an interesting style. You want the reader to grasp the meaning of your work without needing to read every word.

Some people write the way they talk—you can almost hear their voices. Your writing needs to have a "voice" when people read it; otherwise everything becomes just words on paper. Be yourself. Your goal is to say what you need to in your professional voice, in a clear, clean, and concise way.

Just as important as the words you use is the look and feel of the text. The following section will give you ideas for improving the style of your words.

- **Organize first**—Decide what you want to say before you begin writing.

- **Create an outline**—Outline the main ideas of what you want to say; then go into detail on each idea.

- **Use "mind mapping"**—Mind mapping is the process of writing ideas on paper, grouping words and ideas, and clustering ideas in a nonlinear format.

- **Compose at the computer**—Today, many people compose and write at the computer, since they can keyboard information faster than they can write it down on paper.

- **Have a friend take notes**—Talk to someone else and have them jot down notes. This is a great way to start getting organized.

- **Use a conversational tone**—Use a relaxed and informal style of writing. Write in first person, using I, as in I have done this..., I participated in..., I am managing....

- **Use active vocabulary versus passive**—Active vocabulary projects the idea that you are currently working on something. Compare the use of passive words such as **does, get, show,** to active words like **doing, getting, showing**.

- **Avoid slang and too much jargon**—While it may look impressive, colloquialisms may turn what you are saying into code. Remember, the goal is to make everything clear and easy to understand.

- **Tell the truth**—It's always easier to write what you believe and what you have done versus making things up and trying to be impressive.

- **Proof your work**—Proofing your work ensures a professional look and feel to the documents you produce. Spelling, punctuation, or grammar errors can be embarrassing.

- **Use bullet points**—Bullets are an easy way to organize information in a readable, concise way. You've probably noticed after reading through this book that we, the authors, love to use bullet points. Here's a bulleted list of some of the reasons to use bullet points:

Bullets are used to:

- Highlight key points in the text
- Make it easier to quickly scan through information
- List several points or examples
- Eliminate unnecessary text from sentences.

Now, take a look at the same information, written in paragraph form rather than using bullets and decide which is easier to read:

Bullets pull out key information and make it easier for a reader to quickly scan through a lot of information. Bullets are often used when you are listing several points or examples. They also can eliminate unnecessary text from sentences.

Fonts

The look and style of the letters in your documents come from the fonts. Fonts are one of the simplest ways to control the look of your document and can be used to let your creativity and personality flow onto the page.

Serif vs. sans serif fonts—There are thousands of fonts available these days. All of these fonts fall into two major categories: serif or sans serif. Each of these groups has a different look and can be used to emphasize specific pieces of information in the document.

Serif fonts have the little flourishes at the ends of letters. The font you are reading now is a serif font called Bookman. Notice the curve of an "a" or the edges on a "T."

Examples of serif fonts are:

Times New Roman   Garamond   Bookman Old Style

Sans serif fonts don't have the flourishes and curves in the letters.

Examples of sans serif fonts are:

Arial   Humanist   Dom Casual   Tahoma

Decorative fonts—Be careful when you use decorative and funky fonts. These can be serif or sans serif. They are great for projects and section pages in your portfolio, but don't use them as main text in a document. They are hard to read. Use them as accent only, and never on a résumé. Examples of decorative fonts include:

Marydale   Party   **Burweed ICG**   Treefrog

Guidelines for Font Usage

There are no strict rules for the use of fonts, but here are some general guidelines:

- **Use serif fonts for body text**—Serif fonts are easier to read because our eyes use the little flourishes on letters to distinguish the letters. Most of the books you read are in a serif typestyle.

- **Use sans serif fonts for headings**—Sans serif fonts are often used for headings and titles rather than text. They are used to capture interest and draw attention to a particular section.

- **Use all caps sparingly**— USING ALL CAPITALS CAN BE DISTRACTING AND HARD TO READ. THE USE OF ALL CAPS ON THE WEB OR IN AN E-MAIL IS THE EQUIVALENT OF SHOUTING.

- **Don't be afraid to experiment with different fonts**—Find one that says something about your personality, be it *elegant*, **bold,** stylish, or **slightly wild.** Just remember, it must be readable. You don't want your reader struggling to see what the text says. If text is hard to read, we usually stop reading and skip to something else, which could cause someone to bypass some very important information about you. Consider using this type of font in the title or heading section.

- **Don't** mix too *many* fonts together *in* a document—Try to stick to one font for text and another for headings. Your work can look jumbled if you use too many variations.

- **Bold and *italic*—**The same goes for **bold** and *italic*: Use them sparingly, when you need something emphasized.

- **Avoid underlining text!**—Underlining is a tool that was used in the era of the typewriter, when we didn't have bold and italic. Don't use it.

- **Use a proportional font**—Speaking of typewriters, have you ever noticed how every letter on a typewritten document takes up the same amount of space? Proportional fonts will take up less space, let you fit more on a page, and are easier to read. In the sample below, both paragraphs are set in 12 point size, but the nonproportional looks bigger:

  ```
  This text is an example of a nonpropor-
  tional font. Every character or space takes
  up the same amount of space, and it takes a
  lot of space to say something.(Courier)
  ```

  This text is an example of a proportional font. Each character takes up as much room as it needs. (Bookman)

- **Leave only one space after a period**—Remember the typing rule about leaving two spaces after a period? Two spaces were used so you could easily see the end of a sentence in the typewriter age. With the advent of word processors and proportional fonts, we don't need the extra space. You may think it's a hard habit to break, but it is actually very easy to do.

- **Choose the correct font sizes**—The size of the font also affects the readability of the document. The most common size is 12 point. This book is written in 12 point font to make it easy to read at a glance. Ten point is the smallest size we recommend using on résumés and other documents. Any smaller, and it is very hard to read. The text in footers and headers can be smaller than 10 point, as long as they are still readable.

- **Watch the size of headings**—Most headings are printed in 16 to 18 point. Make sure your heading isn't too big for the text; meaning, don't combine 18 point headings with 10 point text.

- **Use spell check**—All good word processors contain a program to check spelling. Use this to correct typing and spelling mistakes. OK, this is an obvious step, but it's amazing how many documents we see where this simple, convenient step was overlooked. Typos look bad (especially on the front page of your portfolio!).

- **Don't rely on the spell checker**—Proof your work. Too many people rely on the spell checker to catch all their mistakes. Unfortunately the spell checker can't recognize words that are spelled correctly but misused in a sentence.

  (You no that I'm talking about, don't ewe?— You **know w**hat I'm talking about, don't **you**?)

Margins, Tabs, and Spacing

The margins, tabs, and spacing you use in a document will change depending on what you are producing. Keep in mind how the document will be used when setting up the page.

Here are some general rules:

- **Single space your text**—You're probably familiar with single and double spacing. Double spacing is commonly used for reports, but single spacing should be used for most of the documents in your portfolio. Generally, you leave a double space between headings and the body of the text.
- **Use a generous margin around the page**—Allow a generous margin around your page, generally 3/4" to 1" around the entire page. Don't make your margins any smaller than 1/2", or your page will look crowded. Many people like to make notes in the margins of a résumé during an interview, and good use of white space in the form of margins allows this. Wider margins also give documents a clean and open look.
- **Don't be afraid to go to a second page**—Two or three balanced, open pages look much better than one cramped page. Keep in mind the information in your documents should be important. Don't go to two pages when you can trim out unnecessary details.
- **Get to know your word processor**—Look for the easy ways to center and indent information.
- **Keep the style consistent**—Decide on a look and style for your portfolio documents and then stick with it. Use the same margins, fonts, and spacing on these documents.
- **Use customized line spacing**—If you "get into" designing the look of your documents, you may discover that a double space after a heading is too much space. If you really want to customize your document, play with settings for the space

above or below the text. This command is often found in the same location as the single or double spacing commands and can be used to add extra spacing before or after a heading.

Which of the following combinations looks best to you?

Work Philosophy: *(single spaced)*
I believe that every person should receive excellent customer service.

Work Philosophy: *(double spaced)*

I believe that every person should receive excellent customer service.

Work Philosophy: *(6 points)*
I believe that every person should receive excellent customer service.

Headers and Footers

Headers and **footers** are areas of text that appear at the top and bottom of a page, outside the normal space used to enter information. Headers and footers are used to print text that should appear on each page of a document, such as page numbers, dates, titles, or names. In this book, the page numbers and the chapter title appear in the footer. If you are planning to duplex a document (print on both sides of a page), you should use the **mirror margin** settings to have information in your headers and/or footers appear on the opposite sides of a left- and right-facing page.

Header and footer information is entered separately from regular text, and usually has tab settings preset to print information left-justified, centered, or right-justified on the page.

Text placed in a header or footer should be in a smaller font, usually 7 to 9 point. You may want to print a line between the header or footer and the main body of text to keep them separated. Here's an example of a page with footers:

```
┌─────────────────────────────────────┐
│  Heading                            │
│                                     │
│  a;sdlkfjaslfasd;lfkasjd;a;         │
│  a;akdjflakd;falksdlsklds           │
│  a;lskfjakjadlksjdaiejle;liej       │
│  a;lsdifasifaslfeifalea;sfehi       │
│  a;ldkfafeias;fiefnefiefnlis        │
│  a;lfiealisejlaieja fie efeifflie   │
│  ;lkjlkjlsdfjaieja;lifjaelieff;     │
│  aife iefeif ejfiaef;alsife iefj    │
│  ;alkjlakaieaslifefisefie asie      │
│  a;lkfjaslf slfkjsfljs ssl sf; slf  │
│  ;lkjaliefj idfjle;slfekajsd;flkja  │
│                                     │
│  Michael Heroux   Feasibility Study │
│  Pg. 10                  4/26/03    │
└─────────────────────────────────────┘
```

■ **Include your name and the page number on each page**—If
  your document is two or more pages long, include your name
  and a page number in the header or footer of each page.

White Space

You'll hear graphic designers and desktop publishers constantly babbling about the correct use of white space. No, white
space isn't the inside of a padded cell or blizzard conditions in
the Midwest; rather, white space is the unprintable area that
appears in and around the text and graphics on a page.

When you make the margins wider in a document, you are
increasing the amount of white space on the page. Take a look
at some of the computer manuals and documentation you've
got lying around, and you'll see lots of variations on the use of
white space. A page which has narrow margins and lots of text
can be tiring to read. A page with too much white space can
make a reader think he or she is missing information. When
possible, add graphics and pictures to a page to add interest
and give the reader's eyes a break.

Here are some examples showing the use of white space on the page:

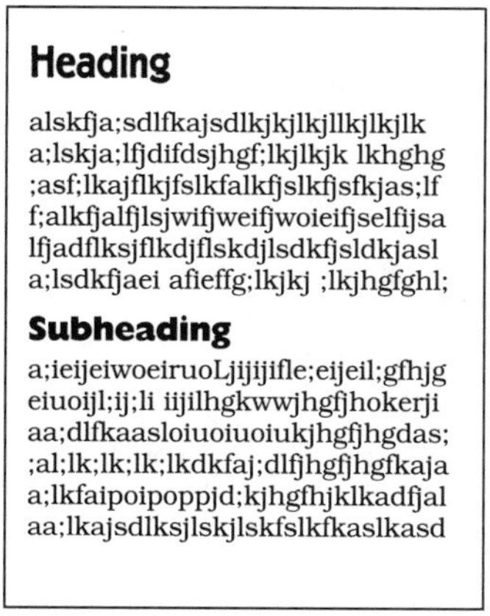

Heading

alskfja;sdlfkajsdlkjkjlkjllkjlkjlk
a;lskja;lfjdifdsjhgf;lkjlkjk lkhghg
;asf;lkajflkjfslkfalkfjslkfjsfkjas;lf
f;alkfjalfjlsjwifjweifjwoieifjselfijsa
lfjadflksjflkdjflskdjlsdkfjsldkjasl
a;lsdkfjaei afieffg;lkjkj ;lkjhgfghl;

Subheading

a;ieijeiwoeiruoLjijijifle;eijeil;gfhjg
eiuoijl;ij;li iijilhgkwwjhgfjhokerji
aa;dlfkaasloiuoiuoiukjhgfjhgdas;
;al;lk;lk;lk;lkdkfaj;dlfjhgfjhgfkaja
a;lkfaipoipoppjd;kjhgfhjklkadfjal
aa;lkajsdlksjlskjlskfslkfkaslkasd

Heading

a;lkj lkldskjfaldkkj ;lkj;lkfja
akdjfdls;j jkj a;lkj;lkjlkekfjk
sdflasjflskdfslfjwiefjlseifjesl
dflkjasdlfjwoioifjaslfselfejal
sd;lfjasdfliajfleijsldijsklifjsefi
a;slkdfjas;lkj;lkj;lkj;;kjkasa

Subheading

lkdgjie;lkj ;lkjl;dlkj kfjeiqoe
eieji;lkj;lkjrkj lkjeejaseifjieji
a;lsdkfk;lj;lkj;ljhkjhald ksdf
a;dkjhkjh;lkj;lkj;kkajsflakjf;a
;fafaklijijlijlilikjlliefj;efiasjliejfe
dslkfjaslfkjaflasedfasdkfjas

Figure 1 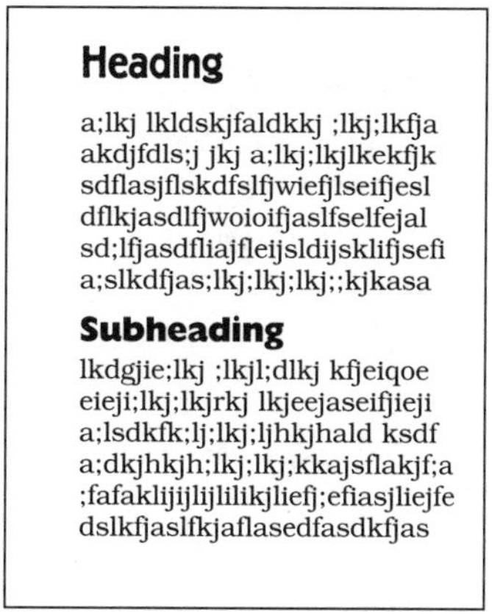   **Figure 2**

Figure 1 contains very little white space and looks cramped.
Compare it to Figure 2 where we added a wide left margin.

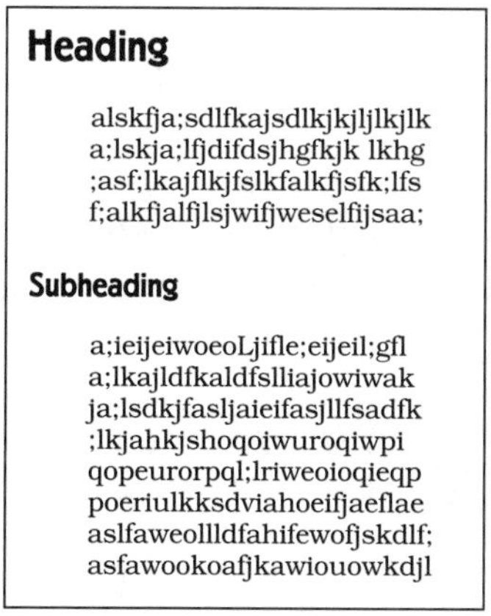

Heading

alskfja;sdlfkajsdlkjkjljlkjlk
a;lskja;lfjdifdsjhgfkjk lkhg
;asf;lkajflkjfslkfalkfjsfk;lfs
f;alkfjalfjlsjwifjweselfijsaa;

Subheading

a;ieijeiwoeoLjifle;eijeil;gfl
a;lkajldfkaldfslliajowiwak
ja;lsdkjfasljaieifasjllfsadfk
;lkjahkjshoqoiwuroqiwpi
qopeurorpql;lriweoioqieqp
poeriulkksdviahoeifjaeflae
aslfaweollldfahifewofjskdlf;
asfawookoafjkawiouowkdjl

Figure 3

Figure 3 adds side headings to the text to make the headings
stand out.

Heading

alskfja;sdlfkajsdlkjkjlklkjl
jas;lskja;lfjdi;lkkjk gfas;dl
;asf;lkajflkjfsfjsfkjas;lfklfa
f;alkfjalfjljwoieifjselfijsalfi
lfjadflksjlsjlsdkfjsldkjasld
a;lsdkfjaffkj ;lkjhgfghl;aeij

Subheading

a;ieijeiwoifle;eijeil;gfhjgfge

Figure 4

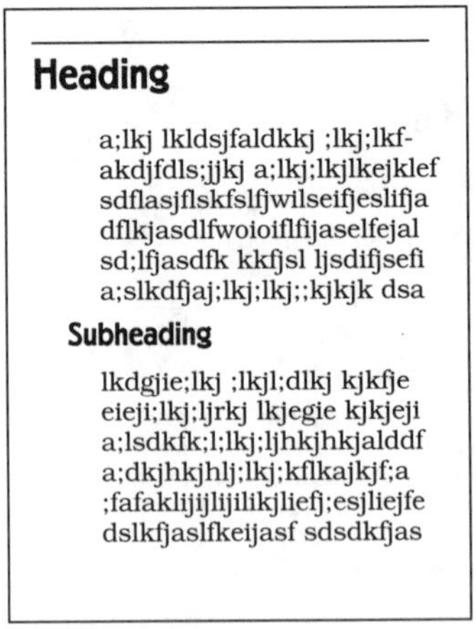

Heading

a;lkj lkldsjfaldkkj ;lkj;lkf-
akdjfdls;jjkj a;lkj;lkjlkejklef
sdflasjflskfslfjwilseifjeslifja
dflkjasdlfwoioiflfijaselfejal
sd;lfjasdfk kkfjsl ljsdifjsefi
a;slkdfjaj;lkj;lkj;:kjkjk dsa

Subheading

lkdgjie;lkj ;lkjl;dlkj kjkfje
eieji;lkj;ljrkj lkjegie kjkjeji
a;lsdkfk;l;lkj;ljhkjhkjalddf
a;dkjhkjhlj;lkj;kflkajkjf;a
;fafaklijijlijilikjliefj;esjliejfe
dslkfjaslfkeijasf sdsdkfjas

Figure 5

Placement of graphics is another important consideration in the use of white space. Keep pictures aligned with text or centered as in Figure 4. You can also add interest to a page by adding accent lines as in Figure 5.

Visual Media—Working with Pictures and Video

A picture is worth a thousand words. It is very important to get your pictures to look their best in order to convey the right impression. There's no question that we learn more quickly from pictures than from words on a page. Like anything else in your portfolio, pictures and videos should demonstrate your ability to perform a specific skill or competency and should be used when words won't convey this or would take too long.

Photographs

Photographs are used to emphasize your work. Take the best shots that demonstrate your work, but don't include too many photos. Photographs can be useful when you want to:

- **Display a finished product**—elegantly decorated cakes, displays, or booths you have created
- **Put your talents on display**—public speaking, training sessions, anywhere you are in action.

Tips for Taking Better Photographs

■ **You should appear in the photo when possible**—This provides proof that it's your work, not someone else's.

■ **Pay attention to film speed**—100 speed film is good for outdoor shots where you don't need a flash. When shooting indoors, use 200 or 400 speed film and use a flash.

■ **Get close**—Get close to your subject (unless you're photographing wild animals!). Use a telephoto lens to get closer if needed.

■ **Fill the field**—Use the field finder on the camera and completely fill the picture with the product. Again, get close to the subject!

■ **Watch where you stand**—Don't shoot pictures into light. The light meter of a camera adjusts for the brightest light, often making the real subject of the picture too dark.

■ **Watch your background**—Most people look a little strange with a flower arrangement for a hat or a pole growing out of their head!

■ **Be prepared**—Try out the equipment before you have to take the picture (i.e., know how the equipment works before a critical moment, so you don't forget to take off the lens cap or find out you have dead batteries in your flash!).

■ **Use a tripod**—Tripods keep your work steady and prevent blurry pictures.

■ **Consider getting a special camera holder**—If you will be taking lots of still shots of products sitting on a table, make a $35 investment in a camera holder specifically designed for taking overhead pictures.

Using Video

Video can be used when you want to show examples of yourself in action. Video takes pictures and adds sound. Keep in mind that no one really enjoys watching home videos, so keep your video short, to the point, and make it worth watching. Limit your video to 3-, 5-, 10-, or 20-minute segments. No one is going to sit through more than a 20-minute video.

Tips for Better Videos

- **Tips for photos also apply to video.**

- **Emphasize your skills**—Keep the emphasis of your video on your skills, not on your production abilities.

- **Be prepared**—Always test out equipment ahead of time, especially if you are borrowing the equipment. It's always good to have extra batteries and an extension cord handy.

- **Watch your lighting**—Make sure the lighting is correct.

- **Label the video**—Indicate the subject and the length of video clips.

Tips for Looking Your Best in Front of a Lens

Your looks:

- **Get a good night's rest**—Weariness and stress are visible. Makeup can only cover so much.

- **Make sure your hair looks neat and attractive**—If you need a haircut, get one several days in advance.

- **Gentlemen, be careful shaving, avoid scrapes and cuts**—Watch out for "five o'clock shadow."

- **Women**—Wear makeup as usual. If you wear heavy liner on your lower eye lid—go lightly or avoid it so you do not look like a raccoon.

Clothing choices:

- Wear a proper fitting suit and shirt.

- Darker tones make the body look thinner.

- Avoid navy blue—It shows everything and appears murky.

- Avoid wearing black and white in color photos.

- Avoid turtleneck shirts and sweaters.

- Avoid wearing a white shirt—It can produce a glare.

- Wear a suit jacket for a serious look—Button the top button on all double-breasted suits.

- Make sure your clothes are not too tight—If you have recently gained weight, a new larger shirt will mask the gain better than a tight-fitting outfit.

- Neckties should look conservative unless the tie is part of a uniform look.

- Keep your jewelry to a minimum.

Production Tools—Copiers, Scanners, and Printers

Copiers, scanners, and printers are the most common tools you'll use to produce your portfolio. Here are some tips for making their output look as good as possible:

Copiers

- **Clean the machine**—Take a bottle of glass cleaner and a cloth with you the next time you go to make copies. Clean the glass on the machine and your final copies will be much clearer.
- **Align the paper**—Center the page on the copier and make sure the paper is straight on the copier. Nothing is more annoying than crooked copies!
- **Enlarge small fonts**—If the original document is in 10 point or smaller type, you must enlarge it to make it easier to read.
- **Copying small pieces of paper**—If you're copying something smaller than 8.5" by 11", be sure to put a white piece of paper behind the document so the background is clear. If necessary, tape the original to the paper to hold it centered. If you are trimming the copy from a larger size, be sure to use scissors. Think neat.
- **Color copying**—Color copying is expensive. Look at the project and determine if you really need color in your work sample. Use color copying when you want to accent something special.
- **Consider scanning as an alternative**—It's hard to copy photographs, except black and white. You should scan color pictures for higher quality.
- **When in doubt, ask for professional help**—The staff at copy centers are usually happy to assist you with your copying.

Scanning Equipment

- **Scanning is often a good alternative to photocopying**—It can produce a clearer picture. Combined with a color printer, it can also be a cheap alternative to color copying.

- **Resolution**—Scanning is measured in dpi—dots per inch. The higher the dpi, the more detailed and sharper the picture. Use no less than 300 dpi, preferably 600 dpi or higher when scanning.

- **Flatbed scanners vs. hand scanners**—Flatbed scanners allow you to copy larger areas of information at a time and provide better quality than hand scanners. They provide higher resolution and less hassle.

- **Scan certificates and degrees**—For a better look, consider scanning certificates and degrees; they copy official seals better than a copier.

Paper and Printing

Paper

As you choose the paper you'll use in your portfolio, keep in mind that the main purpose of the paper is to enhance the text and graphics in the document, making it easier to read. It can also be used to distinguish you from other people and can capture a bit of your style. Here are some guidelines for selecting paper:

- **Use high quality, 24 lb. paper**—Heavier weight paper has a better feel and look. It also helps keep printing from showing through to the other side.

- **Don't use fax paper or any type of thermal paper**—Thermal paper will fade and age. Make copies of any faxes.

- **Paper color**—Use subtle colors, nothing harsh. Use the same paper consistently throughout the portfolio. Use color to draw attention to items you want to emphasize or to title pages. Don't overuse colored paper; limit yourself to a maximum of three different colors. White should be your primary color. Make sure your résumé is printed on white paper.

Printing

- **Use a high quality printer**—Good printers can produce 300 to 600 dpi (dots per inch) resolution. The higher the dpi, the higher the quality of the document.

- **Working with inkjet printers**—If you are printing on an inkjet printer, use paper that's been designed for inkjets, or paper that says it's compatible. Inkjet paper is designed to absorb the ink and give you a clearer, sharper image than regular laser jet paper.

- **Color printing**—Use color printing sparingly to accent important information.

Tabs and Cards

Here are some ideas to keep in mind when creating the tabs and work sample overview cards used in the portfolio:

- **Buy standard size products**—Avery brand labels are the most popular brand. Most word processors can automatically set up a document based on common sizes of Avery brand labels. If you buy another brand of labels, be sure they have the same label measurements as the Avery brand. Most word processing packages have preset templates which lay out the page's margins and space. Setting up labels can be as simple as entering a number from the box. Check out the supply list in Chapter 9, Resource Guide, for specific product numbers.

- **Watch the product's box to see if it is designed for laser or inkjet printers**—If you are printing on an inkjet printer, get the product designed for the inkjet. It is usually brighter and has a coating designed to hold the ink and dry very fast. The ink may spread on products designed for the laser printer. In general, laser and inkjet products are interchangeable, but don't go to all that work and find out the end product looks sloppy.

Follow the guidelines in this chapter and you're sure to have a fantastic looking portfolio! Putting the effort into making your portfolio look professional will pay off in your interviews and reflect the quality back onto you.

Send Us Your Success Story

Our research continues. We are interested in your stories about using a portfolio. We want to hear your experiences and opinions. Tell us how your friends and family reacted. Let us know what you did to improve the portfolio's layout or contents. Share with us how you used the portfolio with your employer and how your organization reacted.

We are interested in the types of work samples you used and how you produced quality copies. Tell us what you would like to see developed or improved in the portfolio. Our next book will have expanded coverage of the electronic portfolio. If you have any questions, ideas, or comments we would love to hear them. Let us know how we can help.

Please send your success story to:

Learnovation® LLC
My Portfolio
PO Box 502150
Indianapolis, IN 46250

or e-mail us at: portfolio@learnovation.com

Visit our web page to learn more about career mechanics and other people's portfolio experiences.

http://learnovation.com

Chapter 9

Resource Guide

This resource guide contains the following materials designed to help make the development of your career portfolio easier:

1. **Supply List** - Materials to purchase.

2. **Emergency Instructions for Portfolio Assembly** - When you need to put together a portfolio fast...

3. **Action Verbs** - A list of verbs used when describing what you have done. Typically used on your résumé and in goal setting.

4. **Department of Labor SCANS** - A listing of general skills and competencies. Useful when setting up skill sets and looking up résumé language.

5. **Transferable Skills** - A listing of skills you can use in many different jobs and situations.

6. **Templates on Diskette** - A listing of the files included on the diskette that accompanies this book.

1. Supply List

Take this list with you to the office supply store. You can also find these items on the Internet at **http://www.officemax.com** or **http://www.officedepot.com** or **http://www.staples.com**

- **Plastic file tote box** (1)
- **Hanging file folders, standard file size** (20–30)
- **Zippered 3-ring notebook** (preferrably leather or simulated leather)
- **Clear sheet protectors** (50–100) Different weights are available:

  Avery 74130 - Diamond Clear© Sheet Protectors - Super Heavy-weight, Top Loading - 50 sheets per box

  Avery 75530 - Diamond Clear© Sheet Protectors - Standard Weight, Top Loading - 25 sheets per package

  Avery 74097 - Diamond Clear© Sheet Protectors - Economy Weight, Top Loading - 75 sheets per package

- **Connected sheet protectors** (3–5 sets)

  Avery 74301 - Bound Sheet Protector Sets - Clear, 10-page set

  Avery 74300 - Bound Sheet Protector Sets - Clear, 5-page set

- **Multicapacity sheet protectors**—If you want to include a magazine or a project that you would pull out of the sheet protector to view, you can purchase multicapacity sheet protectors which can hold 50 pages in each protector.

  Avery 74171 - Multi-Capacity Sheet Protectors - 25 sheets per package

  Avery 74172 - Multi-Capacity Sheet Protectors - 10 sheets per package

- **Extra-wide 3-ring tabs with labels** (1–2 sets)
  There are two different types of tabs available: Tabbed sheet protectors and extra-wide paper tabs.

  Tabbed sheet protectors: You can insert a title page into each tabbed page.

  Avery 74160 - Protect 'N Tab ™ Tabbed Sheet Protectors - Clear 5-Tab, Single Set

Avery 74110 - Protect 'N Tab ™ Tabbed Sheet Protectors - Clear 8-Tab, Single Set

Extra-wide paper dividers:

Avery 11221 - Worksaver® Extra WideTM BIG TAB Insertable Tab Dividers - Laser/Ink Jet, 5-Tab Clear, 3-hole punched

Avery 11222 - Worksaver® Extra WideTM BIG TAB Insertable Tab Dividers - Laser/Ink Jet, 8-Tab Multicolor, 3-hole punched

Avery 11223 - Worksaver® Extra WideTM BIG TAB Insertable Tab Dividers - Laser/Ink Jet, 8-Tab Clear, 3-hole punched

Avery 11220 - Worksaver® Extra WideTM BIG TAB Insertable Tab Dividers - Laser/Ink Jet, 5-Tab Multicolor, 3-hole punched

- **Blank sheets of business cards** (10 sheets)

  Avery 08371 - Ink Jet Business Cards - White, 10 cards per sheet

  Avery 08471 - Ink Jet Business Cards - White, 10 cards per sheet

  Avery 05911 - Laser Business Cards - White, 10 cards per sheet

- **8-1/2" x 11" plastic photo sheet holders** (2–3 as needed)

  Avery 13403 - Photo Pages - Eight 3-1/2" x 5" photos per page

  Avery 13407 - Photo Pages - Four 3-1/2" x 5" horizontal photos per page

  Avery 13406 - Photo Pages - Four 4" x 6" horizontal photos per page

  Avery 13401 - Photo Pages - Six 4" x 6" photos per page

- **Nameplate or vinyl card holder**

  Avery 73720 - Self-Adhesive Business Card Holders - for 3-1/2" x 2" business cards.

- **Paper (high quality)**

  For inkjet printing: use 24# bright white paper

2. Emergency Portfolio Instructions

I Need a Portfolio Now!!!

"Oh, it won't take that long to put it together."

"I have one that I used last time."

"My interview is tomorrow and I have to do all this before I can start on my portfolio?"

"Do I update my portfolio, or do I sleep and shower?"

If you've just purchased this book and want to put together a portfolio for an interview tomorrow morning, or if you've had this book for a while and suddenly your interview is upon you, there's still hope. Based on several frantic experiences of our own, rest assured you can put together a basic career portfolio in three hours if you have a computer, printer, and your best friend's help.

Run to the Office Supply Store and Buy...

- Zippered 3-ring binder
- Clear page protectors (a box or two of 50)
- Extra-wide page tabs
- Plastic stick-on business card holder for front of portfolio
- High quality paper
- Extra ink cartridge (if you're using an inkjet printer).

Grab Your Best Friend and...

- Your box of work samples or file of projects
- A computer and printer
- Your most recent résumé.

We can't stress enough the importance of having a friend help you with the assembly process. Friends can help you make wise choices for work samples, determine your management philosophy and goals, stuff paper into page protectors, make up tabs and exhibit cards, and help you through this somewhat frantic time. A good friend serves as a sounding board and tends to ask questions of you that you wouldn't think of yourself.

Include These Sections in Your Portfolio

- Work Philosophy
- Career Goals
- Résumé
- Skill Areas—Determine different areas. Place work samples in appropriate areas
- Letters of Recommendation (if available)
- List of Professional Membership and Awards
- Community Service—Any work samples and letters available
- References.

Don't Forget to...

- Create tabs for each section
- Make up work sample overview cards for your work samples on plain paper.

See Chapters 2 to 4 for specific guidelines for each of these sections.

3. Action Verbs

Action verbs are used in your résumé to indicate the types of actions you have done. Action verbs can be used in present tense to indicate things you are currently doing.

Accomplished	Equipped	Organized
Achieved	Established	Paid
Adapted	Evaluated	Performed
Adjusted	Expanded	Persuaded
Administered	Expedited	Planned
Advanced	Filed	Presented
Analyzed	Furthered	Processed
Assessed	Gained	Produced
Assisted	Generated	Programmed
Authorized	Guided	Provided
Budgeted	Handled	Recommended
Built	Helped	Reduced
Chaired	Implemented	Repaired
Combined	Improved	Reported
Communicated	Increased	Researched
Completed	Initiated	Reviewed
Composed	Instructed	Revised
Conducted	Interviewed	Screened
Coordinated	Introduced	Served
Created	Learned	Set up
Delegated	Led	Simplified
Designed	Located	Strengthened
Developed	Maintained	Supervised
Directed	Managed	Supported
Displayed	Maximized	Taught
Edited	Modified	Trained
Employed	Motivated	Typed
Encouraged	Negotiated	Updated
Enhanced	Operated	Wrote
Enlarged	Ordered	

4. Department of Labor SCANs

Here is a list of baseline skills and competencies established by the Department of Labor, known as SCANS. Use this skill list to review and organize your own skill sets or to assist in writing your skill descriptions for your résumé.

The Foundation—Competency Requirements:

Basic Skills	Thinking Skills	Personal Qualities
- Reading - Writing - Arithmetic - Mathematics - Speaking - Listening	- Thinking creatively - Making decisions - Solving problems - Seeing things in the mind's eye - Knowing how to learn - Reasoning	- Individual Responsibility - Self-esteem - Sociability - Self-management - Integrity

Competencies—Effective Workers can Productively Use:

Resources	Interpersonal Skills	Information

Allocating:
  - time
  - money
  - materials
  - space
  - staff
	- Working on teams
	- Teaching others
	- Serving customers
	- Leading
	- Negotiating
	- Working well with people from culturally diverse backgrounds
		- Acquiring and evaluating data
		- Organizing and maintaining files
		- Interpreting and communicating
		- Using computers to process information

Systems	Technology
- Understanding social, organizational, and technological systems - Monitoring and correcting performance - Designing or improving systems	- Selecting equipment and tools - Applying technology to specific tasks - Maintaining and troubleshooting technologies

From SCANS—Secretaries' Commission on Achieving Necessary Skills. 1991, U.S. Department of Labor

5. Transferable Skill List

Verbal Communication

- Perform and entertain before groups
- Speak well in public appearances
- Confront and express opinions without offending
- Interview people to obtain information
- Handle complaints in person over phone
- Present ideas effectively in speeches or lecture
- Persuade/influence others to a certain point of view
- Sell ideas, products, or services
- Debate ideas with others
- Participate in group discussions and teams.

Nonverbal Communication

- Listen carefully and attentively
- Convey a positive self-image
- Use body language that makes others comfortable
- Develop rapport easily with groups of people
- Establish culture to support learning
- Express feelings through body language
- Promote concepts through a variety of media
- Believe in self-worth
- Respond to nonverbal cues
- Model behavior or concepts for others.

Written Communication

- Write technical language, reports, manuals
- Write poetry, fiction, plays
- Write grant proposals
- Prepare and write logically written reports
- Write copy for sales and advertising
- Edit and proofread written material
- Prepare revisions of written material
- Utilize all forms of technology for writing
- Write case studies and treatment plans
- Demonstrate expertise in grammar and style.

Train/Consult

- Teach, advise, coach, empower
- Conduct needs assessments
- Use a variety of media for presentation
- Develop educational curriculum and materials
- Create and administer evaluation plan
- Facilitate a group
- Explain difficult ideas, complex topics
- Assess learning styles.

(continued)

Plan and Organize

- Identify and organize tasks or information
- Coordinate people, activities, and details
- Develop a plan and set objectives
- Set up and keep time schedules
- Anticipate problems and respond with solutions
- Develop realistic goals and action to attain them
- Arrange correct sequence of information and actions
- Create guidelines for implementing an action
- Create efficient systems
- Follow through, ensure completion of a task.

Counsel and Serve

- Counsel, advise, consult, guide others
- Care for and serve people, rehabilitate, heal
- Demonstrate empathy, sensitivity, and patience
- Help people make their own decisions
- Help others improve health and welfare
- Listen empathically and with objectivity
- Coach, guide, encourage individuals to achieve goals
- Mediate peace between conflicting parties
- Knowledge of self-help theories and programs
- Facilitate self-awareness in others.

Create and Innovate

- Visualize concepts and results
- Intuit strategies and solutions
- Execute color, shape, and form
- Brainstorm and make use of group synergy
- Communicate with metaphors
- Invent products through experimentation
- Express ideas through art form
- Remember faces, accurate spatial memory
- Create images through sketches, sculpture, etc.
- Utilize computer software for artistic creations.

Interpersonal Relations

- Convey a sense of humor
- Anticipate people's needs and reactions
- Express feelings appropriately
- Process human interactions, understand others
- Encourage, empower, advocate for people
- Create positive, hospitable environment
- Adjust plans for the unexpected
- Facilitate conflict management
- Communicate well with diverse groups
- Listen carefully to communication.

(continued)

Leadership

- Envision the future and lead change
- Establish policy
- Set goals and determine courses of action
- Motivate/inspire others to achieve common goals
- Create innovative solutions to complex problems
- Communicate well with all levels of the organization
- Develop and mentor talent
- Negotiate terms and conditions
- Take risks, make hard decisions, be decisive
- Encourage the use of technology at all levels.

Management

- Manage personnel, projects, and time
- Foster a sense of ownership in employees
- Delegate responsibility and review performance
- Increase productivity and efficiency to achieve goals
- Develop and facilitate work teams
- Provide training for development of staff
- Adjust plans/procedures for the unexpected
- Facilitate conflict management
- Communicate well with diverse groups
- Utilize technology to facilitate management.

Financial

- Calculate, perform mathematical computations
- Work with precision with numerical data
- Keep accurate and complete financial records
- Perform accounting functions and procedures
- Compile data and apply statistical analysis
- Create computer-generated charts for presentation
- Use computer software for records and analysis
- Forecast, estimate expenses and income
- Appraise and analyze costs
- Create and justify organization's budget to others.

Administrative

- Communicate well with key people in organization
- Identify and purchase necessary resource materials
- Utilize computer software and equipment
- Organize, improve, adapt office systems
- Track progress of projects and troubleshoot
- Achieve goals within budget and time schedule
- Assign tasks and sets standards for support staff
- Hire and supervise temporary personnel as needed
- Demonstrate flexibility in crises
- Oversee communication, e-mail.

(continued)

Analyze

■ Study data or behavior for meaning and solutions

■ Analyze quantitative, physical, and/or scientific data

■ Write analysis of study and research

■ Compare and evaluate information

■ Systematize information and results

■ Apply curiosity

■ Investigate clues

■ Formulate insightful and relevant questions.

Research

■ Identify appropriate information sources

■ Search written, oral, and technological information

■ Interview primary sources

■ Hypothesize and test for results

■ Compile numerical and statistical data

■ Classify and sort information into categories

■ Gather information from a number of sources

■ Patiently search for hard-to-find information

■ Utilize electronic search methods.

Construct and Operate

■ Assemble and install technical equipment

■ Build a structure, follow proper sequence

■ Understand blueprints and architectural specs

■ Repair machines

■ Analyze and correct plumbing or electrical problems

■ Use tools and machines

■ Master athletic skills

■ Landscape and farm

■ Drive and operate vehicles

■ Use scientific or medical equipment.

from Life Work Transitions.com

6. List of Templates on the Disk

The accompanying diskette contains files to help you save time while creating your career portfolio. Use these documents as a starting point. Customize these files and make them work for you. Feel free to change the fonts and rearrange information as needed. Each file was created in Microsoft Word 2000.

Faculty_Employer bios.doc - A contact list of people who are mentioned in your portfolio

Memberships.doc - A listing of your professional memberships

Recommendation request.doc - A sample letter for requesting a recommendation letter

References.doc - List your references and their contact information

Skillset.doc - A blank skill set serves as a starting point for creating checklists of your skills

Stmt of originality.doc - A basic statement indicating that the portfolio is your property and should be respected

SWOT Analysis.doc - A worksheet designed to help you plan your career

Work philosophy and goals.doc - List your work philosophy and career goals

Work sample overview cards.doc - Business card layout for printing overview cards used to identify work samples and materials in your portfolio

Directory: e_portfolio - HTML pages that can be edited to create your own electronic portfolio. Files include:

default.htm (home page)	skill_area3.htm
philosophy_goals.htm	skill_area4.htm
resume.hm	community_service.htm
skill_area1.htm	awards.htm
skill_area2.htm	

Index

T

tabbed areas 81–82

tabs 5, 11, 135, 141

templates

    electronic portfolio 99

    faculty employer bios 76

    listing of 148

    memberships 55

    Microsoft Word 40

    recommendation request 62

    references 78

    skillsets 68

    statement of originality 84

    SWOT analysis 32

    work philosophy and goals 23, 25

    work sample overview cards 60, 85

text 121–130

    elements of 123

    fonts 123–127

    headers and footers 127–128

    margins, tabs and spacing 126

    tips for using 122–123

    white space 128–130

transcripts 74, 75

transferable skills 14, 27–28, 64

    community service 72

    examples 28

    list of 144–147

U

U.S. Department of Labor SCANs 143

V

video 131–133

    tips for appearance 132

    tips for clothing 132–133

volunteering 6

W

want ads 69

websites

    job search 48

    résumé 45

white space 128–130

work experience 36

work philosophy 5, 10, 11, 13, 21–23, 25, 32, 83, 84, 141

    defined 21

    sample 22

    using during interview 112

work sample overview cards 11, 57, 84–85, 135

    sample 60

work samples 6, 10, 50–63, 82, 83, 118, 140, 141

    awards 71

    certification 71

    class assignments 50

    community service 53, 72

    confidentiality 58

    co-op projects 51

    creating 57

    degrees 71

    diplomas 71

    electronic 104

    internship projects 51

    keeping track of 58

    letters of recommendation 61–63

    on-the-job projects 51

    overview cards 60

    projects 51

    selecting 57, 82

    skill area 60

    sources of 50–53

    types of 82

    working with 71

    works in progress 65

works in progress 6, 11, 66

ADDITONAL PORTFOLIO RESOURCES

NOW AVAILABLE!

Creating Your Career Portfolio: Practical Exercises Workbook

(© 2003 Learnovation®, LLC) 128 pages. A new companion guide to the Career Portfolio series. This workbook provides nine exercises to guide you through the process of creating your career portfolio. In this book you will take a look at your skills and life experiences and begin to track your experiences, collect and organize your work samples, and discover new skills you didn't know you had. $21.95

Exercises included

1 – Your Career Portfolio Planner
2 – Auditing Job Advertisements for Skills
3 – Class Skills Inventory
4 – Transferable Skills Inventory
5 – Soft Skills Inventory
6a – Planning for the Skills You Need – College Plan of Study
6b – Planning for the Skills You Need – Jobs
6c – Planning for the Skills You Need – Transferable Skills
7a – Résumé Development – Résumé Organizer
7b – Résumé Development – Using Keywords in Your Résumé
8 – Gathering, Sorting, and Refining Work Samples
9 – Creating Your Career Portfolio – Assembly Checklist

Audio Tape

Career Smarts—Career Portfolios with a Can Do Attitude!

This audio tape features an interview with Anna Graf Williams, overviewing the contents of a Career Portfolio and the process of creating and assembling a portfolio. Anna focuses on how to select your best work samples, use your transferrable skills to your advantage, and get that job, raise, or promotion you deserve.
45 min. $15.95

Portfolio Kits

Looking for a fast and easy way to create a portfolio? If browsing through an office supply store isn't your favorite thing, you're in luck! We have three different kits containing all the items needed to create a career portfolio with impact! - We offer three versions of the career portfolio kit: Basic, Standard, and Deluxe.

Each kit comes with a copy of Creating Your Career Portfolio: Practical Exercises.

Basic Portfolio Kit - $28.95
- Plastic 3-ring binder box w/clip
- 10 sheet protectors
- 1 sheet of blank business card (10 cards total)

Standard Portfolio Kit - $34.95
- Tabbed, zippered accordion file for quick organization of materials
- Self-closing 3-ring notebook with five tabs
- 25 sheet protectors
- three blank business card sheets (10 cards each)

Deluxe Portfolio Kit $64.95
- Zippered 3-ring cloth binder
- 50 sheet protectors
- One plastic business card holder for cover ID
- Two 3″ x 5″ photo holder sheets
- One connected sheet protector set
- Two 5-set tabbed sheet protectors
- Two high capacity sheet protectors
- 3 blank business card sheets (10 cards each)

DON'T WAIT TILL THE LAST MINUTE!

Visit our website at **www.learnovation.com**
Call 1-866-332-5905 or fax your order to **1-317-598-0816**

CAREER PORTFOLIO VIDEOS

Career Portfolios are changing the way people interview by helping people plan, organize, and document their work samples and skills. Using a portfolio can help you get a job, get a higher starting salary, show transferable skills, track personal development, and position you for advancement.

Now, three videos are available to help you make the most of your portfolio. Each tape features advice and tips from the experts and takes a look at how real people use portfolios to advance their careers.

Creating Your Career Portfolio – Assembling Your Portfolio

This video overviews the career portfolio process and focuses on gathering supplies, work samples, and materials to include in a career portfolio. This video features interviews with professionals and students who have used the portfolio, tips from the experts, and detailed guidelines for putting together your own portfolio. 25 min. - $99.

Creating Your Career Portfolio – Using your Portfolio in Your Job Search

Once you have created your personalized career portfolio, how do you actually use it in an interview? This video features sample interviews and expert commentary to show the do's and don'ts of portfolio use in an interview setting. Learn tips on using the portfolio to your best advantage. 25 min. - $99.

Transferable Skills – Using Everything You've Got to Advance

Learn how to identify and use your transferable skills to advance your career. This video focuses on how you can use the same skills in different areas of your life. 25 min. - $129

Buy Videos #1 and #2 for $179 and get a free copy of the At-a-Glance Guide! Three video set with a free At-a-Glance Guide book - $299

TO ORDER

Visit our website at **www.learnovation.com**
Call 1-866-332-5905 or **fax your order to 1-317-598-0816**

Mail orders to:
Learnovation® LLC
PO Box 502150
Indianapolis, IN 46250

Shipping:
$0-$99 - 7%
$100 and over - 6%
Indiana State Residents please
  add 6% sales tax